The Tension of Citizenship

PRIVATE MAN AND PUBLIC DUTY

The Tension of Citizenship

PRIVATE MAN AND

PUBLIC DUTY

H. Mark Roelofs, Cornell University

RINEHART & COMPANY, INC. • NEW YORK

To Ann

PREFACE

An examination of the concepts and values clustered around the term "citizenship," and of their condition in American social beliefs, reveals a critical inability on the part of traditional social philosophies to express and defend our heritage of privacy and freedom for individual citizens in modern conditions.

The argument developed in support of this thesis is worked out along the following lines. Chapter I attempts, by cursory examination of various but usual ways in which the word "citizen" is used, to show that in his citizenship the Western democrat is committed to a diversity of sometimes conflicting values. Yet, it is argued, he cannot resolve these conflicts by abandoning one or more of the values which occasion them. As a democrat, he needs all the major values included in the concept of democratic citizenship and can only hope to maintain, at best, an uneasy balance between their conflicting demands. The next two chapters are devoted to an examination of what these values in democratic citizenship are. Three major ones are identified and, as a technique of exposition, are examined within the historical contexts in which they originated.

The first one dealt with is the Greek or, more precisely, the Periclean citizenship ideal, which has come down to modern times almost unchanged. It demands, not on grounds of efficiency but on those of ethical fulfillment, participation in the full range of communal life. The second pattern of citizenship stems ultimately from early Hebraic traditions and amounts, in sum, to an insistence that the "citizen" is a member of the "nation" to the extent that he serves loyally, together with his fellows, in the pursuit of the communal mission. If he does not so serve, he is to be condemned—and again the grounds, being moral and religious, have little immediate relevance to criteria of practicality. These two patterns of citizenship, the Greek and the Hebraic, the rationalist and the voluntarist, both bind the citizen *to* his community. They are treated together in Chapter II.

Chapter III attempts the task of abstracting from a very long period of development the anatomy of an individualism which received its first complete expression from Augustine. This individualism is held to have two major doctrines: first, that all men have a private occupation, private in the sense that the good to be achieved by its pursuit is to be measured in personal terms and not by reference to any public consequences that may result; second, that all men are members or "citizens" of a universal brotherhood, this citizenship both transcending and limiting any present citizenship in an actual community. The two doctrines are held to be indispensable to each other, and no modern Western theory of individualism can be complete without

containing elements from them both. The major consequence of these doctrines is an insistence on some measure
of independence for each citizen *from* his community.

Modern democratic citizenship is an uneasy combination
of these three patterns, the Greek, the Hebraic, and the
Christian-Roman. The final two chapters of the book first
examine the unhappy situation in which this "definition" of
citizenship is to be found in modern society, particularly in
America, and then attempt to erect a new, more adequate
exposition and defense of the concept than what has been
provided by older philosophies.

In the first of these two chapters, it is argued that all
three of the ancient components of citizenship are present
in our immediate heritage but that, in recent years, the two
that bind the citizen ever more closely to his community
have been increasingly emphasized. The third component,
the Christian-Roman pattern of individualism, has been
much neglected. Moreover, the traditional philosophies by
which Americans, popularly, have attempted to express
and justify their social values are no longer capable of ex-
plaining or defending this pattern with the vigor and consistency made necessary by the complexities of modern
life.

The final chapter begins by insisting upon the importance of the ancient pattern of individualism to the democratic way of life and goes on to examine some of the prerequisites for its possible resuscitation in modern conditions. Of special prominence here is the conclusion that the
demand for personal rights for private citizens will have to
be put in far more flexible terms than is customary in this
country. And this demand will have to be based on a revived and clear appreciation of what it is that the citizen
is supposed to accomplish through the possession of his
rights. The argument is summarized by an attempt to re-

write, or, rather, to translate into more usable terms, one of the most familiar statements defending the liberties of the private citizen, the opening sentences of the Declaration of Independence.

There is in all this a bias in favor of privacy and freedom so obvious as to require no comment. But there are other prejudices in this book which may not appear so obvious nor, to some minds, so defensible. Of these much the most important for me is the assumption made about the significance of ideas as operative factors in the social life of man.

Such an assumption may strike the reader, in view of the tenor of much of current scholarship, as naïve, or even, perhaps, as pitiable. On the other hand, it may seem so in accord with plain common sense as to be self-explanatory. My assumption is that man may usefully be regarded as a thoughtful creature, that ideas matter, that to have the "right" ideas is, in fact, essential to anything other than the purely fortuitous fulfillment of purposes. And "purposes" I intend to be taken strictly. My use of the word necessarily implies that man is capable of setting before himself, as an "object" of the mind, a future "good," which he can then seek to achieve by deliberate "decision" and "intelligent" behavior.

To put the matter another way: it is assumed that the questions "What do I desire and how am I to get it?" and "What ought I to do and why should I do it?" are distinct questions and that *both* of them are meaningful. Because of this premise, I have concluded that it is meaningful to write a book about democratic citizenship from the point of view which insists upon considering man as moral and his state and community as moral also, and not as merely sociological phenomena.

The importance of an assumption of this type to a book

such as this one is inescapable. In effect this book, in its limited and specialized area, is a kind of political handbook. With more unkind intent, it might be classed as a book of good advice, a sermon in fact, on citizenship. I admit the attempt is to give, in a sense, good advice, although I hope to avoid the excesses of exhortation sometimes associated with the pejorative use of "sermon."

I do not believe that I am over wary in stating my case in these terms. Political philosophy no longer attempts boldly the task traditionally assigned to it. The study of Hobbes appears to be vastly more popular than the study of those things which Hobbes studied. Political philosophers do not study much political philosophy; they study the history of the subject. They seem to be genuinely uninterested in the question to which Rousseau hoped to furnish an answer: "What can make it legitimate?" On the other hand, they show no hesitation in tackling the question about which Rousseau said he knew nothing: "How did this change take place?"

The temptation to debate the question of the proper function of the study of political theory, is very great. I allow myself only the following paragraphs, and these more in the belief that the viewpoint there sketched is descriptive of the way in which the material in this book is presented, than in the hope of answering potential critics.

The general approach of most modern historians of ideas is well illustrated by the opening sentences of George Sabine's justly famous book:

This history of political theory is written in the light of the hypothesis that theories of politics are themselves a part of politics. In other words, they do not refer to an external reality but are produced as a normal part of the social *milieu* in which politics itself has its being.[1]

But social relativism may be, as Mr. Sabine himself points out, of two sorts. It may be cultural *determinism*. If that viewpoint is adopted, I agree with Mr. Sabine when he says

The substitution of the belief that there is a determinate order of evolution or historical progress for the belief in rational self-evidence displaced an unverifiable idea with one still less verifiable.[2]

To this I would add that there is a certain irony in the enthusiasm with which so many of the empirically minded cultural scientists embrace determinism as the starting point of their work. It takes no great philosophical perception to see that any kind of absolute determinism postulates an order encompassing all history, future as well as past, which is no less nonverifiable on empirical grounds than any rejected Hegelianism.

The other sort of social relativism is indeterminate. It simply supposes that it is convenient to mass everything together and to relate all to one in what is for us the simplest possible way. My objection here is that this approach relegates human values to being "always the reaction of human preference to some state of social and physical fact."[3]

As Mr. Sabine is elsewhere vividly aware,[4] such an approach makes all question of choice between values strictly and purely a matter of intellectual indifference. It renders the man who adopts it incapable of consistently and earnestly disapproving of those vices which, he supposes, his culture has bred him to disapprove. In critical situations, this can be dissatisfying.

I am prepared to agree to the utility of cultural relativism as a technique of historical inquiry. One would have to be unpardonably prejudiced to deny it. To assume that we modern Western democrats are so "because of the history of the West" is an inescapably useful assumption if we are to gain a true appreciation of the values to which we are dedicated. But this should not blind us to the fact that it is only by denying the exclusive validity of that assumption, that it is only by radically shifting to new assumptions, pronouncing those values true and good in some way more universal than any cultural relativism will allow, that we can satisfy ourselves in maintaining them, and in preparing to make such sacrifices as their defense may require of us.

There is one other area of personal belief involved in this book about which there may be some legitimate curiosity. Religion and religious matters are of great concern throughout and some may wonder, therefore, what my own religious convictions are. The question is substantively irrelevant. In this book I am primarily interested in the fact of Christianity in our heritage, not its validity. The facts that the Bible existed and exists, that our fathers back through the ages were Christians in the main and that they used their faith as the final source of moral justification, that the Christian challenge was a problem of the first importance for them, are all facts which I consider to have been vital in determining the nature of the citizenship and political democracy which we now must defend. The majority of modern historians of political ideas have been, I think, both startlingly and dangerously neglectful of these facts[5] and, for my own purposes, I have tried to bring to them some of the attention I think they deserve. But if, after this, there is still question about my particular religious convictions, I can only say that I cannot yet give a clear-cut answer even to myself. I find certain versions of modern Christianity meaningful and have tried hard, therefore, to understand them. That, no doubt, commits me up to a point. It is clear that I write from within the generality of the Christian tradition. But beyond this point I am not yet prepared to go.

On the question of style, there is a point which might well be mentioned here. Political philosophy, as such, is an abstract business, but the more important and significant the discussion of it becomes, the closer it moves to the very warm and concrete domain of everyday politics. There is a constant temptation—some might even say "need"—to illustrate the arguments of political philosophy with examples taken directly from current affairs. The examples are certainly everywhere at hand, but to use them is difficult. Nearly always, even the simplest of them involve a number of major issues, and it is not easy to maintain attention solely on that one which happens to be pertinent. Further, such illustrative material often does more than illustrate: frequently it serves as provocative invitation to hot debate—and debate about the illustration, not the principle behind it. For this point, at least, I am willing to provide an example. A principle of political philosophy upon which much of my argument rests is that the state must provide the conditions which make morality possible. Such abstractness cries out for examples of the kind of "condition" which I, as a supporter of this principle, have in mind. If I suggested "schools" as one such condition, little comment, probably, would be occasioned. But if I added as a further example "soup kitchens," there would be trouble. Though no one might challenge my principle, some readers would instinctively protest that "that kind of thing" poisons all sense of self-reliance. Others would insist that the state should always act with such forehanded vigor that public charity of this sort would never be necessary. In the end, we would all part enemies and, to boot, quite forgetful of our basic agreement. I wish to confine the argument of this book, which is contentious enough by itself, to the principles of democratic philosophy and not extend it unnecessarily to the problems of wise application. It is true, of course, that application, by a kind of feed-back process, often is a proper and determining factor in the molding of principle. Where I have felt this to be the case, I have provided what I took to be suitable illustrative material. But other than this I have deliberately refrained from giving very much illustration to my argument, however much my own political opinions tempted me to insert it. As a result, this book regularly requires the reader to make the serious and imaginative effort necessary to supply the text with concrete, illustrative detail. Equally as a result, the reader has been left free to supply such detail in the light of his own political bias.

Beyond all these comments, I wish to admit and gratefully acknowledge my very great debt to the work of a group of recent and contemporary English political philosophers of whom perhaps the best known are T. H. Green, A. D. Lindsay, and Ernest Barker. The influence of these men, while very great in their own country, has not yet been extensive in the United States. But the lessons they teach are of particular interest to Americans, especially in their emphasis on the pervasive character of society and, with that emphasis, the distinction which in a democracy must be drawn between society and the state. Society, on this view, is that noninstitutionalized community of agreement which arises when men resolve to live together in certain ways and for the better pursuit of certain ends. The state, on the other hand, is that formal organization whose role, whatever the necessity for its authority and power, is that of a servant to society. Of perhaps even greater importance, these Englishmen can impress upon us—through their examination of the ultimate basis of political obligation—the profoundly moral interpretation which the democrat must give to his citizenship, his society, the state, and its laws.

To those who know the work of these Englishmen, their influence will be evident throughout many sections of this book. But before the "labels," those categories which so often do more to mislead than to identify, get too firmly applied, I think it only fair to point out, for whatever they may be worth, certain important differences between myself and these men. For example, the analysis of the nature of rights, given in Chapter V, goes somewhat farther than Green took the problem and also differs in certain important ways from the analysis of it given in his *Lectures on the Principles of Political Obligation.* I also rely much less than Green did on his principle for determining the limits to be placed upon the activities of the state, namely, that the state should provide the conditions without which the citizen cannot act morally, and no more. I am willing to accept that principle for determining the form in which the question "What ought the state to do?" must be put. But I am most certainly not willing, as Green apparently was, to accept that principle as a means for answering the question. I hold instead that this question can only be answered by reference to the moral commitments of citizenship, to what I call hereafter the citizen's "three occupations." This difference in turn raises what is a basic divergence between myself and these English liberals.

This book is written from a "traditionalist" point of view which insists that the moral commitments of the democrat are a consequence of his history and that, therefore, the nature of those commitments is only to be discovered by historical analysis. This leads to the "discovery" that the democratic citizen has these three, often contradictory, occupations: to participate in the life of his community, to serve loyally in its historic mission, and to go his own way in search of private destiny. In contrast, the English liberals I have cited appear to assert that man, by his nature, is a social animal. For them, the obligation of each citizen to participate in his community springs from this moral fact. They then infuse into this Aristotelian approach the point of view of a Kantian, Christian morality so that the obligation to participate in communal life is transformed from an intelligent into an ethical pursuit. These consequences are all commendable except for the fact that they have tended to blind all the members of this English group to what I hold is the divergent and permanently contradictory character of modern democratic citizenship. Citizens are expected to participate but they are also expected to be loyal. More important, they are expected to have private ends, the accomplishment of which, I hold, has no immediate relevance to the state or society. It is particularly in connection with this last point that I hold that Green and Lindsay and Barker have been neglectful.

I wish to take this opportunity to express my gratitude to some of the many persons whose patience, interest, encouragement, advice, and, in some cases, persistence had much to do with making this book possible. First among these is Professor Clinton Rossiter, Cornell University. He was determined from the beginning that I should write this book, had much to do with creating the opportunity for me to do so, and then saved me from many wrong turns as the writing progressed. For detailed criticism of the manuscript I am especially grateful to my father, Professor Howard D. Roelofs, University of Cincinnati; my brother, Professor Gerrit H. Roelofs, University of New Hampshire; Professor William H. Riker, Lawrence College; and Michael Curtis, Yale University. To Professor Herman Brautigam, Colgate University, I am even more in debt. He, too, supplied me with voluminous comment and correction after a careful reading of the manuscript. But even more, as director of the Core 5-6 program at Colgate University, a program in which I had the enviable opportunity to teach, he was a source of both challenge and instruction. He continues to be that for me and for all who know him. I must also thank my typist, Rosalind Steinschneider, for unfailing cheerfulness and efficiency. But, as is always and fairly the case, though all these persons and others not mentioned are largely responsible for whatever merits this book may have, I alone am to be credited with its faults.

H. M. R.

Ithaca, New York
April, 1957

CONTENTS

The Tension of Citizenship

PRIVATE MAN AND PUBLIC DUTY

I

THE MEANING OF

CITIZENSHIP

This book is about the meaning of citizenship, about the special import that word must have for the members of a modern democratic community. It will deal only incidentally with what the laws of particular nations have prescribed with respect to the rights and the duties of citizens. It will deal not at all with those conditions, laid down in intricate profusion, under which citizenship may be gained and lost. There will be little description of political institutions and hardly more evaluation of their efficiency. What this book will aim to do is to elucidate the social and, above all, the moral content of the concept of democratic citizenship.

This, surely, is a proper purpose for a book. But has it not been done? In fact, has it not been done to death, particularly for those young Americans who have fairly recent contact with the public schools? Are we not, most of us, a

1

little weary of being told what it "means" to be a citizen?

The shelves of any public library, even if it is one of only moderate size, will confirm that the literature on "good" citizenship is extensive. Much of it is "educational" in the professional sense. The Schools of Education have made the propagation of the ideal of good citizenship a cardinal mission, and have spread their message through textbook after textbook, lecture after lecture, thesis after thesis. The publications range from "Civic Education in Elementary Schools as Illustrated in Indianapolis" and "The Validation of a Technique for Measuring Certain Aspects of Civic Attitude of 9th Grade Pupils" to *Patriotic Citizenship*, a textbook for elementary schools, and *The Duk-Duks, Primitive and Historic Types of Citizenship*.[1] "The Schools," they consistently declare "are responsible for the Civic competence of their Students." [2]

Political scientists, as a clan, cannot afford to be condescending about this evangelism. The same evangelical spirit was in large part responsible for bringing to political science in many colleges and universities the respectability of independent departmental status. It is no accident that the standard introductory American Government courses were long motivated primarily by the direct desire to teach "young Americans about their government so that they can vote more intelligently." Today, though an increasing emphasis is given in many of these courses to other interests and skills, there is still strong objection to any shift away from primary concern with good citizenship.[3]

The schools and universities are far from having a monopoly of interest in improving American citizenship practice. Nearly all of America's more prominent voluntary organizations involve themselves in projects, regular or special, to arouse the inert and the apathetic. The League of Women Voters comes most promptly to mind, but the

Daughters of the American Revolution, the American Legion, the Freemasons, the (new) Ku Klux Klan, the Knights of Columbus, the Boy Scouts of America, the YMCA and YWCA, B'nai B'rith, the Chamber of Commerce, Kiwanis, International Rotary—to name only some of the better-known groups—each and all attempt in one way or another to inculcate better citizenship in both young and old. The American Bar Association has a Citizenship Committee and so does the National Education Association. The foundations support various citizenship programs: the Falk Foundation supports the Citizenship Clearing House and the Carnegie Foundation is backing the Citizenship in Education Project at Columbia University's Teachers College. There are endowments at universities for special public lectures to be given by distinguished statesmen on citizenship topics, such as the Dodge Lectures at Yale and the Weil Lectures at North Carolina. And, as might be expected, there is annually proclaimed by the President a Citizenship Day.

The amount of money involved in all this activity must be very large and the energy expended prodigious. How then, it may be asked, and now not a little wearily, can another book on the *real* meaning of citizenship be needed?

It is unkind, but it is not irrelevant, to suggest that the need for further thinking on this subject is demonstrated by the very weariness which the professional preachers of good citizenship so frequently create in their less enthusiastic listeners. That the weariness, not to say cynicism, is prevalent, the improvers of citizenship would be the first to admit. Without it, there would be no work for their organizations. But can they be fairly discharged from their share of the responsibility for this weariness and perhaps cynicism, by the explanation that the unrevived always express a certain disdain for the revivalist? Is it either fair or true to say that the lack of response to the pleas for better citizenship is caused solely by ignorance, sloth, or some other, just as immoral, reason? I think not.

I do not wish to seem to belittle the work of the citizenship organizations and schools. Their successes are considerable and, by all accepted criteria, valuable. That their incessantly repeated message should appear hectoring and monotonous is only natural, a hazard for any professional missionary. But they can be criticized, and here sharply, for their simplicity. They preach a vital truth: that for a democracy to work, citizens *must* participate more than they usually do and more intelligently. Yet that is not all that citizenship means in the democracies of the West. The right to private life, the private pursuit of private happiness, is cherished by the English and French citizen no less than by the American. Citizenship does mean willingness to accept public responsibility; citizenship does mean participation, cooperation, and, above all, service. But it also, and just as truly to all our traditions, means, "Go away, neighbor, and let me alone." As an alien, a criminal, an outsider, I would have to be circumspect, but as a citizen, possessed of the rights such status brings, I may demand: "Be off and give me privacy." There is, in Western democracies, instinctive sympathy and moral appreciation for the man who discovered to his dismay that ". . . 'self government' . . . is not the government of each by himself, but of each by all the rest." [4]

There are serious questions to be asked here and the professional preachers of good citizenship are not wont to dwell upon them. Naturally enough. How awkward would be the peroration: "Friends, let each man, to the fullness of his abilities, participate in the communal life, to the very breadth of its range BUT (!) always and only within the limits set by the necessities of his personal pursuit of salvation as he, and he alone, understands that, SAVE (!) only that such understanding must not involve excess of the reasonable requirements of social peace, good order, and defense." Nearer as this may be to the truth as the West understands it, such talk will not do. "Messages" must be simple, and simplicity we get. But simplicity in matters of citizenship leaves us uncomfortable. That sin of which we are accused is only apathy in part; it includes confusion. Bred to the traditions of our heritage whether we can articulate them or not, we feel, at least, the double pull toward both public duty and private responsibility. Regardless of the simplicity of our language the felt meaning of citizenship retains its complexities. These can be unraveled more frequently and more carefully than they usually are.

Unraveling the meaning of words has become for modern philosophers a well-recognized pastime, and the technique of the process standardized. The most important step is to watch how the word is used in its ordinary context or contexts. This involves, in a sense, playing with the word, imagining and recalling both how it has been and how it might be used. The point of the word-juggling is to discover not just one thing but nearly always two things. First, there is the information which the word is expected to convey. This comprises the word's so-called descriptive function. But many words also possess extradescriptive meanings: in addition to conveying information they also transmit, by customary connotation, emotional attitudes and desires. Thus, in the statement "Vivisection is cruel," the use of the word "cruel" is held to convey not only the information that vivisection deliberately inflicts pain but also the speaker's emotional disapproval of vivisection and, at least to some extent, his desire that it should be generally disapproved.[5]

Applying these techniques to a word like "citizenship" is initially illuminating. The merely descriptive content of the word is surprisingly small. Standing alone, it appears to designate, in a very abstract way, membership and then status for individuals *in* a community. How very important these three points about citizenship are—that it implies, first, membership and then status within a community and that these apply only to the individual qua individual—will be readily apparent soon enough, but it must be admitted that of themselves they convey very little about what citizenship "means." Nor are we taken much further when we draw from these points the obvious conclusions that to be a citizen means to possess certain rights or privileges and certain duties or responsibilities. To discover which rights and responsibilities a citizen ought characteristically to have is not easy if we adhere rigorously to the merely descriptive and informative content of the term "citizenship." Reference to particular communities of particular times might be thought to give concrete answers but such procedure is neither helpful nor appropriate. It is not helpful because the laws relating to citizenship are so varied. It is not appropriate because what we wish is not the statistical average of the rights and responsibilities which citizens do have. Rather what we wish is a normative answer specifying all the rights and responsibilities citizens, as citizens, ought to possess even though it might be that few actual citizens ever had all of them. The most that can be said on this score is that the citizen has a status which is to be distinguished, though just how we cannot yet say, from that of the serf, the alien, and the outlaw.

There may be some who will doubt that "citizenship" has this paucity of purely descriptive, nonemotive meaning. Granting the restrictions imposed by the present stage of our technique, still may it not be asserted that the citizen, qua citizen, can rightfully expect to be allowed to vote and participate generally in the political affairs of his community? Is it not, in fact, just these rights and responsibilities which distinguish him from the serf, the alien, and the outlaw?[1]

I admit I am minimizing the purely descriptive meaning of the term "citizenship," but I also must admit that to do this does not seem difficult. "Participate generally" is obviously imprecise, and as for the right to vote, it is essential to ask, "Vote for whom, for what offices and on what questions, how often and under what circumstances?" This is not quibbling. To give the right to vote concrete significance of any importance involves the exercise of judgment within a particular environment. But what is there in the purely descriptive meaning of "citizenship" by which the exercise of such judgment might be guided? I can find nothing there for this purpose. For me, "citizenship," in its merely informative meaning, must remain, therefore, a vague term denoting no more than membership, with status, for individuals in a community.

The story is very different, however, when we turn to the extradescriptive meanings associated with this word. Here there is a plethora of meaning. We can conceive of the statement "I am a citizen" expressing and generating a very wide variety of emotions. It is the presence of these, I am sure, which persuades us that we really mean something when we talk of "the blessings of citizenship." It is these which demand for citizens appreciation for their status in particular environments. It is these, indeed, which give to the term "citizenship" its substance and its complexity. The point of minimizing its purely descriptive meaning was to heighten this contrast, to demonstrate that "citizenship" is a word which derives the greater part of its everyday significance from the fact that our emotions, some of our most poignant longings, are deeply entangled within it.

How important the emotive connotations of this word are can be seen by recalling that emotions can be thought of not only as perturbations of the nervous system but also as dispositions to act in some ways rather than in others. The extradescriptive meanings of "citizenship," therefore, can be thought of as announcements of intentions about future action and demands for appropriate response. "I am a citizen," when interpreted in the full width of its formal meaning, states "I have a certain status in the community," announces "I intend to act in a way appropriate to my concern for that status" and, finally, demands "Let circumstances be ordered accordingly."

To obtain definition of the acts appropriate to the status and of the manner in which the circumstances should be ordered accordingly, the particular emotions that "citizenship" expresses and generates must be identified. If we continue to employ our present technique, we should do this job by playing with the word, imagining various circumstances and various tones of voice in which the phrase "I am a citizen" might be uttered. It takes very little imagination to discover in this way that "citizenship" is definitely a *hurrah*-word, to use the terminology of the philosophers, just as the opposing terms, "serf," "alien," and "outlaw," are all, in varying degrees, *boo*-words. When we talk of citizenship, we talk of something for which we have, habitually, strong, even if mixed, feelings of approval, just as we have been bred from childhood to feel ill-disposed toward outlaws unless they happen to be Robin Hoods.

But to classify "citizenship" as a *hurrah*-word is hardly sufficient. Our feelings of approval find expression in dispositions to act in many other ways besides cheering: we act lovingly or kindly, we worship, adore, protect, serve, join, obey, permit, and so on. Any of these may be occasioned by "a feeling of approval." With which particular dispositions-to-act is the word "citizenship" most characteristically associated?

My own reflection on this matter prompts me to list here three emotional attitudes as characteristically associated with current, ordinary use of this word. These find favor with me for other reasons besides my experience with the word-juggling technique. In fact, they are listed here in an order which foreshadows the results of a very different kind of analysis to be presented in later chapters. But I have used the word-juggling technique, perhaps mainly, to test my conclusions, and I would have the reader do the same.

It seems to me that the most obvious emotional attitude with which "citizenship" is associated is that of pride, pride of place, pride in being a responsible member of a community. "I," we can imagine a man saying proudly, "I am a citizen" and meaning by that "I am the kind of person who is and ought to be an active participant in the important affairs of my society" His intentions are clear: he will keep a finger in the pie, no matter how grubby you and I may think that finger to be. The emotional attitudes he would have his announcement engender in us are equally clear. He demands from us respect, and that we be disposed to allow him opportunities of a significance proportionate to his own opinion of himself. If our laws do not allow him to vote in an election he believes to be important, he will demand that our laws be changed. Special treatment? Indeed yes, for *he* is a special person. He is a citizen.

All this is meaningful description which dispels much of the vagueness surrounding the undefined status conferred by the purely descriptive meaning of the word "citizenship." It provides grounds for that judgment which is necessary to give the title of citizen concrete significance in a particular environment. It also sheds light on the attitudes which the citizen will have toward his fellows. If we inform our proud friend that we also are citizens, he will grant us, if he is consistent, that same respect which he claims for himself. If we suggest that we are government authorities, he will treat us as public servants, with emphasis on the second half of the phrase, for is he not master in that he makes, or helps to make, the decisions which the authorities are supposed merely to execute? But if, to take a final instance, we claim to be superior to him, to have a higher social status, this he will not lightly brook. In a community of citizens, no man is more than a citizen—though many may be less.

Pride in citizenship is for Americans probably the most familiar emotional attitude attached to this word. They can be expected, therefore, to be very nearly as familiar with some of the other emotions into which pride in citizenship can be transformed by circumstances. To pick unhappy examples, pride in this sort of thing can lead to complacency, or, perhaps, to an overkeen competitive spirit, or, quite possibly, to Babbittry. Of more interest is the transformation which occurs when pride in citizenship and the actions in which that would seek expression are thwarted. Then comes anger and, as easily, defiance. "I am a citizen, a citizen, mind you, so. . . ." No doubt, this may be thought of as merely pride aroused and, as simply emotion, it might well be so described. But the disposition to act which would give this emotion expression is quite different from that previously said to emanate from plain pride in citizenship. Then the attitude was positive, the intention to act, in a sense, already decided upon. Now, with this thwarted, a new attitude takes its place, the negative, defensive attitude of defiance.

This may seem a small point but by worrying it a bit we can see that actually it is a very large one. We know from history of many examples of citizens who, having fought and secured rights by defying authority, then fumble badly in the process of deciding what to do with them. Moreover, what is at issue behind the attitude of defiance is not just an attempt to secure opportunities to participate, however much it may appear to be that. What is fundamentally at issue is a matter of sovereignty: who will decide whether the citizen will participate? The right to free assembly, once secured, does not decree that there will be assemblies. It simply allows the citizens to assemble or not as each of them happens to decide. What lies behind the attitude of defiance, therefore, is a demand for privacy of decision. "I, as citizen, will decide whether to go to the assembly and will make that decision according to my own lights." There may be other objects claiming attention: dishes to be washed, money to be earned, God to be worshiped. Any of these may receive priority from the citizen on particular occasions and at the expense of participation in public affairs. Such are the rights and such is the disposition of the citizen—defiant. He will insist on settling for himself both what he will do and when he will do it.

Now that we have come upon it, we can see that the attitude of defiance is a separate and distinctive one. It may be, and often is, directly related to the emotion of pride in participation. But it also may not be and, in substance, it asserts something very different. Proud participation implies community *with*, but defiance in defense of privacy of decision implies isolation *from*. True and full participation, no doubt, requires a large measure of independent and individual initiative but the result must be social union. On the other hand, the citizen who "stands on his rights" not only defies but also declares his personal independence from his community. Defiantly, he is proclaiming the inviolability and sufficiency of himself, of all that is his and of his way in life.

But pride and participation, defiance and privacy of decision do not exhaust the range of emotions and dispositions-to-act distinctive to the extradescriptive aspects of "citizenship." When we conceive of his community strained by crisis, we must imagine the good citizen motivated and disposed in ways not fully explained by the emotions and dispositions thus far discussed. When his community is threatened, the good citizen is neither full of pride nor defiant toward his neighbors; rather, he is aroused to unselfish cooperation by the sentiment of loyalty. Nor is he, if the word is used strictly, disposed merely to participate; his attitude is better described by saying that he is willing to serve, to subordinate himself, and, with that, to surrender much of his privacy.

There can be no doubt that those bearing the title of "citizens" are expected to serve, but there may be real doubt as to whether this service is distinctive of the word "citizenship" as such. Serfs, slaves, and, to use a more challenging comparison, subjects, are all expected to serve. From this it may be concluded that the citizen, as citizen, does not serve. What calls forth service from a man, regardless of whether he is a citizen, is his membership in the community. An analogous situation would be where men obey their fathers and do so without reference to the fact that, besides being sons, they are also husbands. The obedience arises out of the son-father relationship and is, even at most, only indirectly related to the matrimonial relationships. The reason why, this argument might continue, we so easily think of citizens *serving,* an activity quite out of character with the essential meaning of "citizenship," is that modern states so often employ the status of citizenship as a convenient criterion for determining from whom they will demand service, that is, for determining who are members of the community. A similar confusion might arise in the father-son relationship if the father decreed that he would expect obedience only from his married sons, unmarried sons not being considered yet members of the patriarchate. But it would certainly be wrong to say then that husbands, as *husbands,* had to obey their fathers. The correct statement would be that husbands, as *sons,* must obey their fathers. By the same token, this argument might conclude, citizens, not as citizens, but as loyal members of the community, must serve the state in times of need.

This is a plausible argument but it does violence to what I am sure we all feel to be the character of that status denoted by the word "citizenship." Where does this argument go wrong?

In the first place, there is a fallacy in the implication that because other persons besides citizens have to serve, the service rendered by citizens is not a distinguishing characteristic of their status. This is like arguing that because many animals besides horses have legs, legs are not a distinctive feature of horses. To show that this fallacy has been committed it is only necessary to show that the service and loyalty we expect from citizens arise directly out of their possession of citizenship and not from the accidental feature of their being members of the community.

Earlier, when discussing the purely descriptive meaning of the word, it was maintained that citizenship conferred first membership and only then status on individuals in a community. There is no need yet to emend that definition, but any argument based on an appeal to it would be true by *ad hoc* definition only. After all, citizenship may not confer membership in the community; it may simply presuppose membership and likewise the loyalty which we, later on, come habitually to expect from citizens.

A stronger argument to show that the emotive attitude of loyalty springs directly from the fact of being a citizen is to be seen if we do not quibble too much about whether citizenship confers or presupposes membership in the community. Certainly all citizens *are* members of the community, and service and loyalty can therefore be expected from them. More fruitful for our purposes would be to notice the character of that service and loyalty. Is it distinctive, different from what is expected of other members of the community?

As soon as the question is put in this way it becomes obvious that the citizen's loyalty is of a distinctive kind; it is different because it comes from the kind of persons citizens are assumed to be. They are proud, assume themselves capable in special ways; and they are jealous of their rights of independent decision. The community of which they are members is much more theirs than it would be if they were merely slaves; as citizens, they not only *own* membership in the community; they also possess the community itself in that they, being participants in its decisions, have the use of it to a degree and in a sense denied to aliens and slaves. Thus, the loyalty to be expected from them must be a loyalty freely given, the service they render unhesitating. Anything else would nullify the essential character of their citizenship. The slave must serve always and without question. The subject must be dutiful. And the alien may well do only that which is specifically required of him by the authorities, and no more. To all these the loyalty and service of the citizen stand in contrast. In a very real sense, though all are expected to serve, only he can be truly loyal, only he can *give* service.

The burden of this argument reveals not only that loyalty and service are distinctive characteristics of the status denoted by the term "citizenship" but also that this third emotive meaning of the word is as distinctive as it is very largely because of its association with the other two previously discussed. The citizen's loyalty would not be what we have found it were it not that citizens are citizens, proud and independent. But the extent of the influence should not make us suppose that the third emotive attitude expressed by the word "citizenship" is simply a new form of one or another of the other two. How different in kind the third one is from the others is easily illustrated.

In the early phases of America's participation in World War II, officials in Washington were determined that the vast army then being created would be a characteristically American one. They were determined that it would be, as they called it, "a Citizens' Army." There was something altogether admirable about this attempt, but it did not succeed, of course, and it was soon abandoned. The acknowledgment that the Americans, individually as well as nationally, are a proud and independent people, was simply swamped by the requirements of organizing their free and loyal service into an efficient military machine. In "normal" times, the emotive meaning of "citizenship" which receives most emphasis in America is, probably, the proud one. But in times of crisis, it is forced to give place to other connotations of the same word which are very different and which find expression in very different dispositions-to-act.

The philosopher's word-juggling technique for unraveling the meaning of words has thus taught us a good deal about the term "citizenship." It has forced us to observe the breadth and complexity of meaning associated with this seemingly simple term. In its purely descriptive content, the title of citizen implies membership and then status for individuals in a community. In its extradescriptive meanings, it may convey, depending upon the context, any one of a whole range of emotions and corresponding dispositions-to-act: pride and participation, defiance and privacy of decision, loyalty and service. Each of these pairs is distinct, not identifiable with any of the others, but each seems to have obtained something of its character by being associated with the others within the confines of the one word "citizenship." Finally, and with the greatest relevance to our further considerations, "citizenship" has been shown to be of that class of words which derives its major significance not from informative meanings but from emotive connotations.

Enlightening as these results may be in themselves, their most substantial advantage lies in that they enable us to state in fairly precise and complete form that problem which is hidden behind the fair ideal of citizenship and which was briefly noticed in the introduction to this chapter.

It is now obvious that the citizen is expected to be a certain kind of person. No matter which of the various dispositions-to-act associated with the word is evoked, in every case there is the assumption that the holder of the status of citizen is an autonomous agent, free, independent, capable of self-direction and self-responsibility. If he is to participate, it is he that is to do so. If he is to defend his privacy, it is to secure an area for the free exercise of his independent judgment. If he is to be loyal, he must *give* that loyalty, for the loyalty of the citizen cannot be borrowed, stolen, or taken by force.

But if the free "unitness" of the citizen is obvious, so also is it obvious from investigation into the meaning of this term that the citizen is expected to do a number of different and conflicting things. The conflicts are most apparent when the demands for action are stated in extreme form. Full participation can be achieved only by the abject surrender of privacy, and vice versa. More subtly but with equal difficulty, as we have seen, the attitudes of proud participation and loyal service are essentially different: how can the haughty citizen maintain pride in his place against the demands for total servility? Finally, perfect loyalty to community demands the complete elimination of selfish concern with private destiny. Prima facie, these conflicting claims are each too unyielding for there to be, without real loss, any sublimation of some of them into others. Pride, defiance, and loyalty, when linked to particular dispositions-to-act by word "citizenship," no more mix than does oil with water.

This is most painfully true, of course, when the demands upon the citizen are put in extreme form. In the ordinary course of successful practice it is probable that the citizen maintains such peace of mind as he can through moderation and compromise. He will be reluctant always "to go all the way" with any one of the three sets of claims which citizenship puts upon him if only to preserve his essential character as a free agent and the possibility of serving the remaining two. He will be unwilling to be totally loyal because of the wish to preserve such measure of independence as is necessary to both real participation and privacy. The same sort of considerations will preclude him from entering completely into active participation in the affairs of his community and, on the other hand, from completely retiring from them.

The argument for moderation and compromise is reinforced by the further consideration that, just as the citizen will be unwilling to pursue totally the claims of any one strand of citizenship at the expense of the other two, so also will he refuse to sacrifice totally any one for the better fulfillment of either or both of the remaining two. Should he be so misguided as to make such a sacrifice, he would soon learn that he *needs* all three of the strands. He will find that if he is to maintain some one of the three for which he particularly cares against the impossible claims of one of the others, he will need all the assistance he can get from the remaining third, no matter how unimportant it might otherwise appear. None, therefore, can be abandoned. The possibility of free political participation can only be preserved in times demanding the utmost loyalty by the unrelenting support of the claims for privacy. Under the same conditions, privacy can only be secured by vigorous political action. (We all know that "the price of liberty is eternal vigilance." Have we forgotten that without liberty no vigilance is possible?) On the other hand, if "the sense of community" which only a common loyalty can create is not to be destroyed by the anarchistic tendency of extreme claims for privacy, political participation will have to be encouraged. Nor is this all. If citizens are to enjoy the satisfaction which an active political life can bring, then they will have to be shaken out of a too selfish concern for private affairs by inculcating in them a greater sense of communal loyalty. There is no fun in running for office if the campaign must be conducted in empty auditoriums or if the candidate is badgered at every turn by special interests. No doubt there are further combinations of the facets of citizenship which could be made in this same connection, but the ones given here are sufficient for the present argument. They are also the ones most immediately relevant to the perplexities of our current age.

The conclusion to which all this points is that the citizen simply must use moderation and a willingness to compromise if he is to preserve his status intact. He cannot hope to satisfy the claims of any of the emotive aspects of citizenship completely nor can he afford to neglect wholly any one of them. His only hope is to maintain some kind of balance between them all.

But the way of moderation and compromise, in this matter as in so many others, raises questions, some practical and at least one both serious and theoretical. Would the League of Women Voters be satisfied if a husband remarked that he was quite ready to exercise his political rights of citizenship but only in moderation? Or would a Committee on Un-American Activities give a clean bill to a man who insisted that he was loyal to his country but in a compromising sort of way? Would such a committee be any happier if he went on to explain that, while he did not for a moment contemplate any active disloyalty, yet there were limits, set by himself, beyond which he would not extend service to country? Finally, and in these days this is almost pathetic, how much comfort would we bring to the hard-pressed private citizen if we told him that we were going to defend his personal liberties in a spirit of moderation and compromise? Awkward questions, perhaps, but, if these reflections on the various ways in which the word "citizenship" is used have any merit, all these people with their specialized points of view would have to be content with less than they desire. If citizens are to be citizens, in the sense(s) the word is used, the special pleaders cannot be given more than what compromise and moderation allow.

On the theoretical level, however, is a question which admits of a less ready answer. It is all very well to say that the citizen must strike a balance between the three competing aspects of citizenship. But how? The language is quantitative, but to suggest that we could measure quantities of loyalty or pride or defiance, much less balance them off against each other, is absurd.

A deceptive answer to this question may be provided if we go back to the argument that no one strand of citizenship should be sacrificed because of the necessity of having from each the help it can give to another in defense against overweening demands of the remaining third. It might be held that "circumstances" will show which strand needs the greatest emphasis for the better preservation of community and good citizenship. Therefore, all that needs to be done is to provide that particular emphasis and then to encourage, whatever the circumstances, just enough interest in the other strands to prevent them being finally submerged.

This answer is deceptive because, quite apart from the extraordinary reliance it places on "circumstances" to inform us on questions of value and on the notion, too, that our ultimate object is simply to *preserve* citizenship in all its present confusion, it does not really answer the problem at all. Suppose, as seems to be our present "circumstance," that the community is menaced both by an external threat and by internal subversion. Loyalty is then, quite properly and obviously, at a premium. Both free participation in public affairs and areas of privacy must give place and, as the danger increases, be ever reduced to a minimum. But which types of political action are to be left uncontrolled and which areas of privacy uninvaded? The question is *not* one of who will decide these matters but rather of how the decisions are to be made, and by reference to what criteria. Must we leave it wholly to the needs for security and loyal service to dictate what will be allowed? That would be abject surrender and would disregard that opportunities for free participation and privacy are to be secured *despite* the demands for ever more complete loyalty. It may not be argued here that the demands for loyalty will be self-limiting on the grounds that without freedom the spontaneous loyalty of citizens cannot be forthcoming. If the whole concern is with loyalty and the service it prompts, there will be that much less concern with whether the services actually rendered come from citizens, or subjects, or serfs. In times of communal crisis, the demands for absolute loyalty too easily overreach themselves. Some criteria outside of loyalty, something more durable than its own supposed prerequisites, must be found by which its tendencies toward excess can be held in check.

The question of how much participation, loyalty, and privacy we wish to have in certain circumstances can never be answered by a mere inspection of those circumstances. That will do no more than tell us what the circumstances are. We can only answer the questions of how much participation, how much loyalty, how much privacy we should have in particular circumstances by first answering another question: What is it that we wish to achieve in those circumstances? Once this is known, we can determine the proper amounts of participation, loyalty, and privacy by finding them to be necessary, to be means to the achievement of our purposes. When there is the kind of communal crisis referred to above, loyalty is needed, obviously, but only because in those circumstances what is wanted is to preserve the country from the transformations which alien forces threaten to effect. Putting it more generally, we can say that there are explanations or, better, justifications, for the loyalty demanded, these referring to a good that is desired. By the same token, there are likewise justifications to be had for the demands for political participation and for privacy. Theoretically, at least, it would be through use of these justifications and the goods to which each refers that the amounts of loyalty, participation, and privacy appropriate to particular sets of circumstances would be determined.

The question before us is no longer what does "citizenship" as a word mean: it is now one of why this word has come to mean what it does. Why do citizens wish to be loyal, to participate, and to have privacy? What, in short, are the values which citizens as citizens seek to secure for themselves? If we can discover these, if we can say persuasively why it is that we, as citizens, wish to participate, serve, and yet have still a measure of privacy, we will have gone a long way toward arming ourselves with criteria by which to decide how much of each of these diverse activities we should insist upon being allowed to perform in particular situations.

These general questions, involving all three of citizenship's major aspects, can be given more sharpness if we concentrate them upon the problem of the citizen's privacy. This problem cannot be considered in isolation from those arising from citizenship's other aspects. Privacy is not secrecy. It can only be obtained in useful amounts by the knowing cooperation of a man's neighbors, by the deliberate restriction of social action and social concerns. It must be included within, not excluded from, the normal social pattern. These considerations make privacy at once the most threatened aspect of modern democratic citizenship and the most difficult to defend. Yet I believe, and will try to show later on, it is the most vital to our democratic faith. By no means is it the only consideration, and in my exposition and defense of it I will regularly attempt to give due consideration both to the facts of society and to the authority of society's ideals. But I do hold to the centrality, within democratic citizenship, of privacy and the individualism which privacy allows. Without these, democracy as we know it would be a moral sham.

Hence the paramountcy of the question, Why does the democratic citizen desire privacy? What is it that he must do in the private? And where is the high justification for this attitude of "do it myself, by myself," a justification which can fairly demand at least partial relief from the contrary claims of nation and neighborhood? It is not enough, as we have said before, to point out that the citizen must have some privacy, some freedom from external interference and dictation, if his participation in and service to his community are to be genuine. The citizen does wish to take part and serve freely, whether the community involved is his country as a whole, or the business establishment where he works, or merely the vaguely organized social life of his neighborhood. But surely he claims more freedom than that. No one can suppose that Jefferson, when he wrote the words ". . . and the pursuit of happiness" into the Declaration of Independence, wished to have each of us free to dedicate ourselves to the happiness of this or that or another group. He was claiming, and so do we when we cite him, the right which would allow each of us to pursue our own, our personal happiness. But on what grounds can we claim that right, when state and place of work and social opinion so demand all our loyalty, all our participation, all our attention? It is obvious that limits must be set and enforced by the public authorities to hedge in on every side the means and ends of our private pursuits. It is obvious that our governors, our employers, our friends and neighbors can all make demands upon us. On what grounds can we limit those demands? Indeed, why limit them at all? There is something patently absurd about insisting that our hard-pressed society deliberately honeycomb its fabric with areas of virtual anarchy.

The arguments for society's demands are persuasive. The morality of society and its groups is unselfish, outgoing. The morality of privacy is, at least, egocentric. And it would be so much more efficient, in the short run if not also in the long, if the state not only compelled obedience to the nationally necessary law and morality but also went as far as is humanly practical to harness our personal and so often wayward energies into the cause of the common good. This could be done democratically. There is no institutional bar precluding democratic totalitarianism. Political parties, public debate, even private enterprise and private property could still exist. We would only have to learn to judge and regulate these things by the one criterion of public need. Yet arguments of this sort do not convince us. Rather, they terrify us. Public need and public duty must be limited. The state must be restricted and neighbor told to stand aside even if the cost prove high. I demand and you demand, in spite of the imperatives of modern social life, that some room be left for each of us to be on our own. But why? It is obvious what we wish to be free from. But what do we wish our freedom for?

Before dealing directly with this problem, one further point must be developed with care. The mere examination of the meaning of words, with its search for descriptive and extradescriptive connotations, can be of no further use. This technique has widened the range of our investigation, forced upon our attention complexities in this word "citizenship" which otherwise might have escaped our notice. But it stops short of asking the questions we now feel required to ask. As a technique, it is, in a sense, only two-dimensional: it discovers the meanings of words in their current usage but cannot explain why and how they have come to mean what they do. It reveals that certain words have, in different contexts, different emotional connotations but it does no more than identify what the emotions are. If, as is the case with "citizenship," the emotions are conflicting ones, it can only report the conflict as a fact: here is a word conveying mixed emotions. It cannot teach us much about how to deal with the conflict—or even whether we should.

The technique to be used here in unraveling this conflict of meanings within "citizenship" is frankly traditionalist. I do not wish to be drawn into attempting an ideal or perhaps, in some absolute sense, a perfectly "democratic" solution of what is, after all, only the modern form of the ancient problem of the one and the many. Such a way would be, I am convinced, in the end vain. I assume that the conflict between the opposing values associated with the term "citizenship" is a real one only because it occurs within the historical context in which we live. We in the Western democracies are citizens. We did not become such by the free exercise of some absolutely rational choice between rationally distinguishable alternatives. We were born citizens. In general, my contention is that the only useful solutions to *our* moral conflicts are to be found in the process of rediscovering and re-examining the values and ideals passed down to us from *our* history.

The positive case for the traditionalist approach as a means of solving current problems of political philosophy has recently been persuasively put by Michael Oakeshott. Many of his points are conveniently summed up in the following:

. . . the more thoroughly we understand our own political tradition, the more readily its whole resources are available to us, the less likely we shall be to embrace the illusions which wait for the ignorant and the unwary: the illusion that in politics we can get on without a tradition of behaviour, the illusion that the abridgement of tradition is itself a sufficient guide, and the illusion that in politics there is anywhere a safe harbour, a destination to be reached, or even a detectable strand of progress. The world is the best of all possible worlds, and *everything* in it is a necessary evil.[6]

The first of Oakeshott's "illusions"—that we might be able to get along without a political tradition of behavior— is the classic, Burkean argument for historical prescription. It is the contention that consistent, stable social behavior is very largely dependent on habit, ingrained respect for traditional norms. The maintenance of the historic fabric of a society, granted the desirability of consistent, stable social behavior, becomes a primary task. Innovation and reform must always be marginal and gradual. Revolution is easy, but the production of a common, inherited outlook is the work of generations. Therefore, solutions to such persistent problems as that of the one and the many cannot be, if they are to be socially useful, ideal or even best solutions. Rather, the only possible solutions are to be found within, and appropriate to, an inherited culture.

These arguments for the traditionalist approach are reinforced by a consideration of the second of Oakeshott's "illusions"—that the abridgment of a tradition can be itself a sufficient guide to constructive political policy. The Burkean argument may persuade us that we ought not to attempt to advance without due respect for the past, but it does not by itself go far toward defining the role which the political theorist, as a theorist, should play. Oakeshott is anxious that we should not exaggerate what the theorists can accomplish. They can abstract, that is, "abridge," from the totality of our history, ideals and principles and then present these to practical men of affairs as guides to be followed and policies to be pursued. They can formulate, in short, social ideology. But, Oakeshott warns, the practical men must accept such ideologies with caution and always seek to apply them in actual situations only in the light of their own consciousness of the whole of the inherited past. Abstraction from a history for the purpose of formulating some "time-tested" principle will always and inevitably result in that history being more or less abridged. Yet, surely, what all this serves best to emphasize is the job the theorists can do. Earlier in the lecture from which the above quotation has been taken, Oakeshott found reason to point out that a politics without policy is neither feasible nor, if it were, desirable. He put the point both on the practical level—politicians who indulge in mere vote catching get us nowhere—and on the theoretical level—the *purely* empirical study of political institutions is no study at all. Without a hypothesis (to be tested) or an ideal (to be worked for), absolute empiricism becomes either unself-conscious animalism or lunacy. The traditionalist approach does imply a relatively rigorous empiricism. The materials with which the theorists must work are the factual materials of history. But these materials must be studied. We may agree that the abridgment of history and the principles such abridgment supplies are not sufficient or permanent guides; nonetheless they are prerequisites to political advance.

This is a second argument recommending the study of traditions and, like the first, it is practical in temper. The third is even more so. Oakeshott's final "illusion" was that in politics there is anywhere a safe harbor or even a detectable strand of progress. Then followed the somewhat enigmatic concluding sentence: "The world is the best of all possible worlds, and *everything* in it is a necessary evil." These sentiments are more comprehensible if we again refer to an earlier passage of his lecture. There he described the ship of state as launched, in effect, upon a limitless and bottomless sea. There is no knowledge of whence it has come or of where it is going, or even if these ports exist. All, apparently, that the crew members have to rely upon is their own unaccountable urge to keep sailing and, for purposes of navigation, the records they have kept of their own self-discipline and their charts of past course and speed. This I take to be Oakeshott's ultimate justification for studying the traditional culture with so much care. There can be no justification of political purpose in terms of some fixed, absolute heaven ahead or, for that matter, hell behind. We know only the present and *its* past. So, given the complexities of human aspirations in all their nobility, grace, and humanity, let us get on with it, making full use of the wondrous instruction that history, especially ours, affords.

To the contemporary skeptical temperament this is an attractive point of view for, without doing violence to any of the principles of that temperament, it yet holds up a law to live by.

For myself I cannot challenge any of its essentials. The faith for which we have fought and for which, if necessary, we will undoubtedly fight again is the inherited, traditional faith of our fathers, however much we may from time to time adapt it, restate it, and purify it to make it more acceptable to our modern conditions. We will fight for it because it is in us, it is the source and the judgment of all that we wish to preserve. We are our fathers' sons; that is why we have become who we are, democrats and Americans. But I confess to believing that Oakeshott's justification for accepting traditional values is questionable on two serious counts.

His mood, it seems to me, is quite wrong. He holds his view dispiritedly. It is for him, we can guess, a second-best kind of faith. He would dispel our illusions, as he himself, we can judge if we watch only his choice of phrase, has been disillusioned. There is a hankering in his words for a hard, objective, absolute faith which would proclaim *itself*, without recourse to any subjective element in the discovery and acceptance of it by us. This is a mood for which there must be much sympathy, but it neither becomes nor accurately describes the manner in which we in the West believe in our democracy, our citizenship, the essential values of our way of life. These we believe in not because we cannot find anything else more suitable. The fact of our belief is sufficient evidence that they are for us "good"—not just "better than nothing."

Moreover, Oakeshott's mood obscures—if it does not actually transform into something very different—the character of our attachment to these values. Our outward demeanor is often, and perhaps ought to be more frequently, marked by moderation, skepticism, and understatement. That is dictated by our faith. But our attachment to that faith is nonetheless a dedication of self to service. It is true that for us there can be no dedication without a great element of rededication—but the workaday, academic research which that implies should not transform or obscure the fact that what is involved is yet a dedication.

Our commitment to democracy and its citizenship is very deep. Attempts to justify it in terms of what is "reasonable" and "practical" seem to me to be always wide of the mark. They ignore the fact that what we now accept as being "reasonable" and "practical," to say nothing of "what gives enduring satisfaction," are defined as reasonable and practical by reference to this prior commitment. In truth, though we can know much about how and when the commitment took place, we cannot explain *why* it did. In logic, the question cannot be properly put, because it is the commitment itself which is the ultimate basis for all our justifications. In experience, we cannot begin to know what evidence would provide an answer because the evidence of experience can never justify; it can only elucidate circumstances. But we can be much more aware than we usually are that we have been committed. In the techniques of modern historiography we are fortunate in having means for discovering much of what we need to know about this commitment to the democratic faith which history has thrust upon us.

It is in this spirit that I undertake the present inquiry into the meaning of democratic citizenship and especially of that facet of it which demands respect for the privacy of individuals. I put before myself and my reader the fact, the historical object, of modern citizenship, *our* citizenship. I will try to analyze that object not by reference to some ideal of what citizenship should mean or to what it would mean in a certain kind of good society, but rather by reference to what it has in fact come to mean in our history.

I I

THE CITIZEN AND HIS

COMMUNITY

The various ideas and ideals of citizenship, preliminarily identified as pride and participation, loyalty and service, and defiance and privacy, have rather obvious historical origins, in Greece, in ancient Israel, and in the Christian-Roman world. For the traditionalists, these origins are of the first importance because it was in them that the shape of the modern citizen's commitments was determined. But, once this first valuation of the importance of origins is granted, there are other advantages to be had from a careful examination of the places and manners in which the modern ideals of citizenship came into being. In their originating cultures, these divergent ideals can be seen in some isolation from each other. In concrete situations, we can look at them, as it were, one at a time. More important, the problems occasioned by each of these ideals can be seen unmoderated by the conflict of demands which arise

31

when all three ideals are present, as they are today, in the same culture.

These supplementary considerations are particularly apparent in any examination of the Greek origins of the ideal of participation and of the Hebraic origins of the ideal of service. Both these ideals bind the citizen to his community. But when we examine them separately, we can see that they bind him in very different fashions, and have equally different consequences.

A : THE GREEK PATTERN

Much the most conspicuous of the ideas clustered within the concept of citizenship is that derived ultimately from the Greek, or, more specifically, the Athenian, ideal of political life. It is the most conspicuous, partly because it is the one most consistently associated in Western history with the actual word "citizenship," but also because it is the one which has been least altered by the passage of time. The Periclean Ideal of good citizenship, in very nearly the same terms as Thucydides had the great Athenian put it in the Funeral Oration, has been a familiar source of civic inspiration for nearly twenty-five hundred years. It has, in fact, become so familiar that we now tend to accept it as an ideal without question. Yet, clearly, here is a case where we realize too little that, although the ideal itself has hardly changed, much else has. It is only a slight exaggeration to say that, for Pericles and his fellow citizens, the ideal of city-state patriotism was the one and only ideal deserving wholehearted acceptance. For them, it comprised the whole meaning of "citizenship." For us, on the other hand, that ideal must compete for place, and our acceptance of it can be only partial and compromising.

That the Periclean Ideal is ours but yet neither wholly

nor exclusively to our liking can be shown simply by looking at it more closely than we usually do. And, again, the place to do this is in the Athens where the ideal was born. This was the Athens of the period before too much "democracy" and too much empire drove her citizens into the service of other gods: the golden Athens in whose common life citizens with full pride participated and around whose memory men ever since have placed halos of virtue and respect.

But there is no single body of unexceptionable evidence descriptive of this Athens. Neither Plato nor Aristotle is a reliable witness on what Periclean Athens really was like, for neither fully experienced its life, and both could only look back to it with troubled nostalgia. Thucydides, though closer to it in time, is hardly better, as his views are even more colored by bitterness and regret. Yet these three men, biased as they may have been, are for us in some respects the most important witnesses. The Athens which historically existed and the Athens of Western memory are not quite the same thing, and it is as it appeared within the latter that the Periclean Ideal has come down to us. Plato and Aristotle, with Thucydides playing a lesser role, were the main agents in determining the form which the real Athens would take in our memory. It has been their understanding of the Periclean Ideal, and not so much that of, for example, Pericles himself, which has had the major influence in determining our own modern understanding of it. Modern scholarship in recent decades has insisted correctly that the vision of Athens transmitted by the philosophers is both too narrow and too simple to represent fairly either the Athens that was or the idealized version of it operative in the minds of its own inhabitants. The philosophers grossly neglected especially the breath of understanding which the Greek dramatists displayed about human psychology and morality. With even less excuse, they ignored the significance of the Sophistic tradition of independent criticism upon which they, themselves, as philosophers, built. But, for the purposes of discovering the remembered ideal determinant in Western history, these failings are of only indirect importance, and their correction comes, in a sense, too late. Our fathers and their fathers in turn leaned heavily on the works of the philosophers. When they thought about Greek politics and Greek political ideals they knew no more, except in rare instances, of the wisdom of the Greek dramatists or of the individuality expressed in the life of Socrates than Plato and Aristotle chose to tell them.

None of this is to imply that we can ignore the patient reconstructions of Greek life provided by scholars of our own age.[1] On the contrary, we must rely upon them extensively. Indeed, contradictory as this may seem, we are forced, all in all, to rely upon these modern reconstructions even more than we are upon the works of Plato and Aristotle. The great philosophers were just that, and they did not have reason to set out the Periclean Ideal with the fullness of historic detail which we now wish to recover for it. For this reason alone we would be justified in attempting to get past the philosophers to the historical situation behind their thinking. But there is an even more important reason for doing so. The philosophers set themselves philosophic problems and discussed them in abstract, sometimes utopian terms. But always and most importantly, a major part of the context within which they undertook these discussions consisted of their own knowledge of the actual Athens of their day and their memory of what it had been only a short time before they wrote. As a result, what must be recovered is the real Periclean Ideal of the real Athens. But we must understand this as it would have been understood by the philosophers. Put another way, we must, though with some self-consciousness about what we are doing and why, oversimplify and overintellectualize the Periclean Ideal as it is discoverable in the modern reconstructions of the real Athens. This means, in specific terms, that we will largely ignore the dramatists and poets of Athens. The ethics of civic life will be given a strong philosophical bent and will not include the very great concern which many Greeks had for the sin of *hubris* (pride). Above all, we will neglect the supreme individuality and the tradition of personal honor expressed in the life and death of Socrates. Yet, within the confines of these deliberate distortions, we will attempt to recover in some fullness that ideal of civic duty which grew up in the real Athens.

Clues to the almost instinctive attitude of the Athenians toward political affairs can be found in their vocabulary of politics. Ernest Barker has listed some of the leading terms of this vocabulary for just this purpose. He points out that the most important of these all have, in the original Greek, a common root; our modern corresponding terms do not. And Barker further notes that the Greek words were both less precise and more social, whereas ours are both more strictly and more impersonally legal. The terms he lists are these:

POLIS : the Greek conception of the state (not, therefore, the somber and rather distant thing which is the state for us), the power of the organized, whole community, but also, simply, the community, the city. (*N.B.* The Greeks had a special word, *asty*, to denote the city when referred to simply as a place of residence.)

POLITÉS : citizen, a member of the community and a full participant in its common life.

POLITIKOS : statesman (not "politician" even in our nonpejorative sense implying merely a party professional), a leader in the community.

POLITIKÉ : the theory (or, rather, the art) of the common life of the *polis* and its betterment (not, therefore, fully translatable by our more rigid and formal "political theory" or "theory of the state").

POLITEIA : the constitution, but in a sense including, besides the laws assigning the basic powers of government, the system of social ethics, the way of life.

POLITEUMA : the body of persons composing the citizenry. It is the concrete, personal side of the *polis,* just as the *politeia* (constitution) is its abstract side.[2]

Barker thus summarizes his comments on these terms:

They are terms belonging to a vanished Mediterranean world of "urbanity," which is not our world; and only those who lived in that vanished world could hear and understand the fullness of their music.[3]

There is no gainsaying the general truth of this comment, but it puts the case too strongly. Not only is Barker here underestimating his own very considerable contribution to our present understanding of that lost world, as well as those of the whole brilliant company of English scholars of which he, A. E. Zimmern, Gilbert Murray, F. M. Cornford, and Sir John Myres are only the most familiar members. He is also tending to neglect the fact that the music which these Greek words evoked for the citizens of ancient Athens is still, to no small degree, played for us. Of course, the Mediterranean world of 450 B.C. is a vanished world, but it is not as "vanished" *for us* as, say, the early civilization of Japan. We still have, even if in the more technical, colder Latin forms, our own urbane language of the city. "Citizen" and its immediate derivatives, "citizenship" and "citizenry," are the most obvious relatives, but there are also "civil" (in the sense of "civility" as well as in the adjectival sense of "civilian") and "civilization." And we have "civics," made so familiar by the phrase "civics course" and all that *that* implies. Our family of words does not knit together as neatly as did the Greeks'. But we can see, in the meanings which we give to each of our words, traces of the meanings which the Greeks gave to theirs. Barker is no doubt right to suggest, as a translator, that "statesman" is the best available single English equivalent for *politikos* (even though it connotes more of Woodrow Wilson than it does of Themistocles). But does not the phrase "leading citizen" from our idiomatic speech carry over, philosophically speaking, more of the *full* meaning of the Greek word? Is it not more descriptive not only of the *politikos* and his role in the community but also of the implied values of communal life? It certainly carries over some of this, and that it does so shows that the Greek habit of verbally linking man and neighborhood has not vanished. But the points of difference are also important.

The Greek *polis* words all refer basically to the same thing, the communal life of the civic republic; our *city* words, except in nearly lost root meaning, do not. "Civility" now implies the mannered relations between individual persons; "civilization" implies an advanced culture for a broad mass of people. From the point of view of city life, the first has become too small, the second too large. A second point of difference is that, whereas all the words of the *polis* family are primary terms of the Greek political vocabulary, only one or perhaps two ("citizen" and "civics") of ours are of major importance in our political life.

These differences are indicative of the altered place which the ideal of city life now occupies. The first difference suggests the extent to which we have transferred "urbanity" as an ideal into other areas of human intercourse, and the second the extent to which that ideal has been forced to yield its former place of unquestioned primacy.

Because language so often reflects instinctive value preferences, these points of similarity and difference are more important than casual thought might suggest. But as yet they are hardly more than hints. They can be given substantial support and added significance by evidence taken from more usual sources. If we look from the language to the ideas and institutions which the language described, we can find vivid explanations for the ease with which in Athens *politiké* ("civics"—the art of the common life) was linked to *polités* (citizen) and both to *polis* (the city-state).

In the realm of politics, the practical achievements of the Greeks tend to be overlooked. They are overshadowed by the greater and more durable triumphs in the realms of the arts and ideas. Greek political practice is most usually noted for its astonishing variety of forms. Even so, the Athenians, especially, accomplished a remarkable feat in this field. In the space of a very few centuries, they developed a working system of democratic government which, though limited in both practical scope and territorial extent, was yet a startling contrast to the primitive autocracy from which it sprang. Much of the meaning of the title "Citizen of Athens" was determined by the role which the notion of citizenship played in that development. And it is in this historic role that the explanation is to be found for the intimate connection established in Greek history between the citizen and his city.

Two major obstacles stood in the way of self-government coming to Athens. The first of these was the prehistoric tradition which ordained that the family should be the central and, originally, the sole unit of social organization. The second was the tendency, very common in rapidly developing communities, to entrust the tasks of government to "the few." To both these obstacles, the notion of citizenship was a radical challenge.

Democracy, even in the limited Greek form, implies for those who participate in it, personality and, more importantly, individuality. The citizen is to attend, speak, and vote in the *Ecclesia*, each one for himself. Unless he speaks and votes for himself, there is little purpose in his coming.[4] The same applies to his membership in the great popular courts: if his judgment is not his own, why have *him* give it? But the social organization dependent on the clan denies social individuality. It loses the individual within the anonymity of the family hearth. Crimes are crimes of the blood for which responsibility is taken by the group collectively. The power of any central government will be blocked from control over, or service from, individuals as individuals by *patria potestas*.

In its earliest days Athens had the usual primitive social organization based not on individuals each with status within the community but on tribes subdivided into gens. It is against this background that citizenship first appears. It arises as a never completely successful civilizing idea by which the individual is wrenched free of the multiple attachments of the clan,[5] and through which he is related directly to the state and its laws. It is the idea by which and through which the *polis* comes to have concreteness, to possess both the possibility and the capability of having a "life" of its own. Citizenship was much more than simply a symbol of the shaking off of older, lesser loyalties and of the primacy of newer, greater ones. "A family" is not created just by thrusting under one roof assorted adults and children of appropriate ages. Relationships must be established and acted upon from within: relationships of son, daughter, parents, man and wife. This is the creative role which citizenships plays for the city. It is an idea in terms of which the units of a mere aggregate can be presented as combining into an organic whole. It is never enough to define the citizen in himself as simply "a citizen." He must always be defined *as related* to the city of which he is a member. And it is when, historically, individuals can be and are defined as so related, that "the city" becomes a practical possibility. Before that time, the city, such as it is, can be no more than a confederation of tribes and gens.

Citizenship has frequently played this *civilizing* role, in early Roman history, for example, as well as in ancient Greece. And one further aspect of it deserves serious note. The family, as Hegel would say, is a "community of feeling"; that is, its relationships can be established and, to a high degree of satisfaction, maintained merely by reliance on emotion and instinct. Most families can get along quite well without their members cogitating deeply about the essential natures of their roles in the family group. But the community of citizens, again as Hegel would say, is "a community of understanding." The community of citizens is not only bigger, more complex, and more enduring than the family; it is, perhaps only because of these things, more abstract. To comprehend it, to discuss its affairs intelligently, we have to think, not just feel. Our language reflects this. We find it necessary to talk frequently of "the general welfare," "the national interest," and sometimes, even, of "the common good" and "the will of the people." There is a noticeable lack of corresponding terms for the family.

For this bigger community we not only have to have "laws" (written down) but also symbols (flags, government buildings, political rituals, and pageants) by which those of us who find it difficult to live in terms of abstractions may be reminded of their existence by material representation. Thus "citizenship" is, in a very special and important sense, a "legal" concept. It is legal in the strict sense that a citizen can be compelled to obey law and may participate in its making. But also, and now using law in a more general way to imply simply the order of the state-community, citizenship is legal because it refers to and is only understandable in terms of the abstractions which constitute that communal order.

Citizenship, then, from its very inception, had important meanings quite apart from the duties and rights which eventually came to be habitually associated with that status. On the one hand, "the citizen" was an abstract entity, a personality, an individual. On the other hand, he was related to and "a member" of another abstraction, the "state-community," larger, more complex than the family or tribe, and against which not even *pater familias* could stand. And it ought to be added again that this meaning of citizenship was not peculiarly the contribution of Athens. It is just that Athens, within our recorded history, was the first of our "cities."

Much more indigenous to Athens was the contribution to the meaning of citizenship which resulted from the battle between citizens and "the few" for control of the city. If the contest with the reactionary tribal traditions had given citizenship its form, this contest with "the few" supplied it with content. The fact that these two contests were, in Athenian history, going on simultaneously accounts for the warmth and immediacy of the otherwise abstract relationship between the citizen and his city. Unlike the subject, and the kingdom to which subjects must be loyal, the citizen seeks not only to be a member of his community but also to make it especially his own by sharing in its government.

The victory of the citizens of Athens over "the few" was, for a period at least, complete. The Tyrants were early got rid of and later the *Areopagus* (Council of Elders) was retired to a position of dignified impotence. The Twelve Generals, who largely replaced the *Areopagus,* were controlled, and their subservience to the *Ecclesia* was ensured by requiring each of them to render a personal accounting of his office each year to the assembly. The systematic use of lot, pay, and short tenure guaranteed not only that any citizen could occupy the various other executive offices but also that a very large number of citizens would. Pay and, later when the end was near, fines, in some cases, for nonattendance, meant that the *Ecclesia* lost none of its vitality and, of no less importance, the great popular courts none of their powers. There are few other instances in Western history in which the whole body of citizens—even though this might be only a portion of the total population—so completely obtained control over their government or exercised it with such a consistently high degree of participation.

This must strike us today as a very laudable situation, particularly when we remember that submerged half of our own electorate who so habitually neither vote, nor care, nor, apparently, know. And we approve, too, of the principle which was used to explain and justify it. We may trust that Aristotle, though after the fact, was accurately conceptualizing something in the Athenian tradition when he made, as the premise of his political philosophy, the notion that man, by nature, is a social animal. The family and the village are natural, too, but their functions are to provide for the absolute necessities of mere life. The *polis,* however, is natural in a higher, more spiritual way in that it provides the framework within which the social animal can achieve his *telos,* can develop to the full his highest nature. It was in this sense that the Greeks described the function of the state as "justice" and maintained that it existed to make men "good."

Historians are quick to distinguish, as Thucydides did, between "real" and "alleged" reasons and they will point out that the operative reasons for the rise of Athenian democracy were practical, not idealistic. The citizens did not get from the Tyrants and Oligarchs the kind of government they wanted and they had the wit and the power to take over the government themselves. But we are here less interested in why Athenian democracy arose than we are in the theories in terms of which it was understood and expressed. From this point of view, the Tyrants and Oligarchs were thrown out because they were unjust, and they were essentially unjust to the degree that their monopoly of the government deprived citizens of the opportunity to fulfill *telos.* The cruelties, inefficiencies, and failures of the governments of "the few" were not, therefore, so much bad in themselves as they were symptomatic of an ultimate injustice, the frustration and perversion of "the natural." Only personal participation in the processes of government by all citizens could fulfill the design of nature.

Thus, in the Athenian tradition, citizenship first postulated the individual in a form in which he and his fellows *could* be combined into one whole and then, under the guise of a demand for self-government, proceeded to weld them into that whole by an ethical theory which equated the life of the citizen with the life of the city. But before we examine some of the troubling implications of this definition of citizenship we should take note of the influence which it had, for a time at least, on the Athenians. The evidence of the Funeral Oration is, no doubt, suspect.

Thucydides' generously tinted glasses are between us and whatever it was that Pericles actually said. And, in any case, speeches by generals over the graves of the fallen must dwell much on honor, service, and country and are only too apt to contain phrases like "where the rewards of virtue are greatest, there the noblest citizens are enlisted in the service of the State." [6] But a reading of the Oration still leaves the impression that by modern standards Thucydides has Pericles go to quite extraordinary lengths to defend the city as the primary object of proper devotion. One by one, all other possible objects of affection and loyalty, both social and religious, are assigned to lower place. This is a major reason why the Oration is held to be one of the finest patriotic speeches of Western history. But it is also true that it is in just this respect that it is so much harsher than the Gettysburg Address, a speech to which it otherwise bears a most startling resemblance.

Modern historians also go to some lengths in pushing their unanimous agreement that for the Greek citizen politics was all-absorbing. In our sense of the word, politics is confined to interest in law and government as such. By doctrine and practice, we exclude from it any direct and inhibiting concern with religion, most matters of private morality, and all aesthetic interests in drama, architecture, music, and sculpture. But all of these were, in the Greek sense of the word, political. The Athenian mind could distinguish neither between the state and its society nor between service to the *polis* in its festivals and service to it in its courts.[7]

The point that the *polis* was church, state, and much else besides, all rolled into one object of loyalty, is made poignant by the appearance, after the glory of Athens had begun to crumble, of other notions of the perfect life. In both Aristotle and Plato, for example, the withdrawn, contemplative life of the philosopher is a serious distraction. Though Plato is more famous for the ruthless limits to which he was willing to take the principle of communal duty, yet, in the Allegory of the Cave, there is ample evidence of an unresolved tension between the rival claims of ideas and society. And Aristotle, although in the *Politics* defining man consistently as a social animal, holds in the *Ethics* man to be essentially reason and the life of the philosopher divine. Neither philosopher took any notice of these discrepancies.

A. E. Zimmern, while not talking directly to this point, provides, in a footnote on the use of gardens in ancient Greece, some illuminating evidence for it. "Gardens reveal," he writes,

a desire for privacy which was foreign to the City State. It is characteristic that the first people to make a regular use of private gardens, and to look upon them as indispensable, should have been the philosophers. The Academy and the Lyceum were not so much a training for City State life as a substitute for it. Socrates taught in the market place and in the public wrestling-grounds: Plato and Aristotle "moved out into the country." [8]

The move was characteristic, both of the minds of the philosophers and of what was happening to the old simplicity and purity of the Periclean Ideal. But there is also significance in Zimmern's having taken note of this kind of evidence. Zimmern was an Englishman, and England is at once the most homogeneous and politically organized of modern democracies and a country in which the exclusively private, high-walled, overadorned back garden is the hallmark of the dominant middle-class culture. Modern democrats are at least as reluctant as the ancient philosophers to allow the civic ideal the unquestioned, complete acceptance which it once had in the age of Pericles.

The reasons for this reluctance lie not in the ideal itself. All admit that to be fair indeed. The most usual worry about the ideal itself seems to be usually no more than the practical one of how to fit the "citizen and his city" into the monster political structures of modern times. Our real reluctance about this ideal springs rather from some of its logical corollaries, and from the practical consequences which flow from any attempt to apply it rigorously without the very great modifications which result from the parallel application of other ideals. Most of the, for us, "bad" features of Athenian democracy can be understood as being part and consequence of the, again for us, too single-minded devotion to the communal life of the *polis*.

The most obvious "bad" feature of Greek city-state practice—the consistent and unquestioned exclusion from citizenship of large segments of the population—is a major example of this. In terms of the Greek tradition, to participate was never properly a means of satisfying selfish ambition but was rather an opportunity to contribute to the common life of the *polis*. But if participation is understood in terms of contributions to the common life, it is altogether logical to insist that only those who can contribute in this way should be allowed the opportunity to do so. There is more than a shadow of this argument in the prevalent usage today of the literacy test. You have got to be *able* to vote before you will be allowed to vote.

But the notion that you must be good enough to be a citizen before you can become one is nothing more than an application of a more general doctrine: "From each according to his strength, to each according to his need." And as a general principle, this was very much a part of the

Athenian tradition. Bury tells us that the conservative principle of the almost mythical Athenian lawgiver, Solon, was that "the privileges of each class should be proportional to the public burdens which it can bear." [9] Aristotle, two and a half centuries later, made the same idea the basis of his definition of equality:

In democracies, . . . justice is considered to mean equality [in the distribution of office]. It does mean equality—but equality for those who are equal, and not for all. In oligarchies . . . inequality in the distribution of office is considered to be just; and indeed it is—but only for those who are unequal, and not for all. [10]

From this it follows that while some will be capable of being citizens, others will be thought able to contribute to life of the *polis* only in a menial way. This is, in fact, an essential feature of Aristotle's contention that some men are slaves by nature. It also follows from this notion of " 'equality proportionate to desert' " [11] that criteria must be established and judges appointed by which the merits of individuals can be appraised and their claims settled. Unlike modern democrats, who must always pay some tribute to that other principle of equality, "Each shall count for one and none for more than one," and who therefore feel impelled to keep the standards for admission to citizenship as low as possible, the Greeks had no compunctions about keeping theirs high. Plato would have, in effect, allowed citizenship only to the guardians, the philosopher-kings. Aristotle, who had some faith in the judgment of the mass in assembly, was only relatively more lax. And the Athenian democrats, though they were very "democratic" among themselves, were not adverse to maintaining an exclusive atmosphere. They early restricted citizenship only to those whose fathers and mothers were both of citizen stock and legally wed. They tolerated, with an indifference which shocks their modern admirers, the total and permanent disenfranchisement of not only all slaves and women but also the large body of aliens whose presence in Athens brought so much prosperity to the city.

In our day, not only do we often require the abilities to read and write to varying degrees of proficiency (always to be adjudged by someone), but we also hear from time to time of various schemes of plural voting: ordinary citizens, one vote; citizens beyond a certain wise age, two votes; citizens beyond that age and members of the learned professions, three votes; and so on. And—though the principle remains precisely the same, the practice is usually concealed—the ballot is sometimes effectively restricted to those who are of the "right" race or even to those who "know" enough to vote for "right" candidates.

The Greeks were never so subtle but, perhaps because of their innocence, they were always willing to extend both their practice and theory by a further consideration. Politics is a time-consuming business. To practice it well and to the full requires at least some relief from other vocations. So Aristotle said and so the Athenians obviously thought. Therefore, so that some may be free to be citizens, others must work. And the very fact that these others, slaves, women, and, if available, aliens, must work so long and hard means that, quite apart from congenital deficiencies, they have no time for politics. They simply cannot be citizens. The proponents of plural voting, with identical emphasis on citizenship solely in terms of participation, should take note of this argument. Negative voting in the plural may present certain practical difficulties, but zero voting does not.

There is another side to all this which gave citizenship

a connotation it was never to lose. If citizens are unequal to noncitizens, the principle of proportionate justice will insist on the other hand that all citizens *are* equal, one to another. And this equality within the class of citizens is not a proportionate equality but rather is the equality of sameness. Citizens are all citizens.

The very wide use of lot and short tenure for political offices in Athenian democracy most obviously testifies to suspicion of the ambitious. But it testifies as well to the extent to which the Athenian democrats were willing to assume an absolute kind of equality within their own number. Modern historians stress the presence of this egalitarianism-within-limits. Zimmern is particularly struck by it. He refers constantly to the "club-life" of Athens and maintains that to this day there is more real social equality in the lands of the Near East than ever there was in the great republics of the West where, even so, equality is a major political doctrine. He notes especially the lack of personal ostentation in ancient Athens and the high degree of mutual respect which the citizens showed to each other.[12]

This tendency to practice the doctrine of the equality of citizens in an almost mathematical strictness was reinforced by the proclivity of the Greek mind to define and classify things in terms of "essence," "Man" was of a class, to be defined in terms of his essence, reason or sociability. Individual men, by this approach, shared a common possession of "manness" and, therefore, were all essentially the same. They were all but particular examples of one universal, and their various individual differences from one another were "accidents" and never "essentials"—except, of course, for the exceptions: women were not men, slaves were somehow incomplete men, and aliens were outlanders.[13]

Thus, even at this early date, citizenship took on a hue

which was ultimately to contribute greatly to Western radicalism. Athenian citizenship was radical not only in the sense that it opposed government by the rich and the wellborn. It was radical in the more primitive sense of implying egalitarianism. It implied government by the many equal. The Athenian citizen was proud, too proud to believe that he might properly have superiors; but he was also rather common. His claims were ever after to make "people of the better sort" uneasy in their privileges and power.

To this aspect of Greek egalitarianism, the modern democrat, especially the modern American democrat, will respond happily. Modern citizenship, especially in America, does challenge emphatically the pretentions of those who claim to be of "the better sort." But the Greek implication that egalitarianism involves sameness is repugnant to our doctrine, however much it might be applied as an accurate comment on our practice. And our unhappiness with this suggestion can only increase when we recall the exceptionally inclusive definition which the Greeks gave to the politics within which the sameness of equal citizenship appeared. In principle, we abhor sameness and cherish rather individuality, by which we often mean simply diversity. Yet the Greek suggestion of sameness in citizenship follows logically enough from the premise which defines citizenship in terms of participation in the communal life. Again we have an instance in which our admiration of the Athenian civic ideal must be marred by dissatisfaction with a perfectly natural consequence of its exclusive application.

If we take all these characteristics of Athenian citizenship together (definition of citizenship solely in terms of participation, very wide definition of politics, a rigid exclusiveness about the citizenship class, and a leveling sameness within it), we can see that they add up to a difficulty which is critical for the modern mind. It concerns the extent to which the Greek citizen was involved in the life of his city and can be best seen when attempts are made to derive from the Athenian tradition a definition of liberty.

These attempts are by no means easy. Liberty, today, has become such a loaded word that calm definition of it for any purpose is now always hard. Any attempt to translate it within the context of Greek culture alone is made doubly hazardous by the almost complete absence from Greek political-philosophic thought of any precise concept of individual will. The concept of the autonomous, self-directing "will," largely Hebraic in origin and of great impact on Western political thought from Roman times onward, is an essential presupposition of the modern notion of the "free man" who deserves to have, because he is supposed to possess the innate capacity to use, the rights of personal liberty. There are substantial grounds for arguing that not even the later Greek philosophers ever really discussed liberty and its problems in our terms. But C. D. Burns and other historians are right, all the same, to insist that the Greeks, despite the lack of the notion of "will," did have *a* concept of liberty and that it has a direct relevance to our political tradition. That concept is also the most complete single expression of the Greek value of citizenship.

Burns suggests that the primary sense of Greek liberty refers not to the individual but rather, as always, to the *polis* to which the individual, as a member of varying degree and capacity, contributes. The liberty of the *polis* is the liberty of "The Free City" and it is closely related to our notion of state sovereignty. In its most obvious sense, it is simply negative: it means merely the independence of the group, as a group, from external dictation. The policies to achieve it are not so much moral and dynamic as defensive, policies of self-preservation for the group. But, in the Greek tradition, these policies were a response to something very moral indeed. They were the expression, to use Burns' words, of "the desire of a group to carry to their full development the character and intelligence which [was] common among them and distinct from that of their neighbors." [14] In the sense of freedom *from,* this liberty, then, is merely conservative. But in the sense of freedom *to do,* this Greek liberty is part and parcel of the general and noble tradition that man must seek his salvation and ultimate satisfaction in the freely developing communal life of his "city." In final essence, this is a most positive liberty: liberty for the achievement of high moral purpose, by the group and within the group.

It is a dangerous misunderstanding to conclude from this concern for the developing life of "The Free City" that the Greeks—and therefore also any of our own day who should happen to share this concern—can be easily condemned for having an idealism appropriate to a totalitarian philosophy in the modern sense. The Greeks, for this, talked too much of individual *telos* (end) and not enough of *telos* for the city. Moreover, some kind of grand-plan view of man and state in history is an essential presupposition of the modern totalitarian approach. It is consistent to demand the devotion of the total energies of every citizen to the common cause only when the whole nation is seen on a divine march toward the achievement of some end external to itself. Visions of this sort seem to be impossible without a deep concern for the whole onward rush of all history. Though the Greek philosophers had a greater sense of history than is sometimes allowed them, yet, just as they had no concept of the individual will, so also did they lack any such over-all historical outlook. Greek philosophers simply did not possess the intellectual context with which the Hegelian (or Marxian) total glorification of the state is a doctrinal possibility. In any event, they had, in the notion of the moral necessity of the achievement of *telos* by the individual "social animal," their own, and for them, completely adequate justification of the state. The role of the state was to make men good, and this had little if anything to do with having the state keep a rendezvous with destiny. The Greek philosophy was one of development toward perfection within a quite timeless theory of order. In it there was simply no room for an all-enveloping theory of progress through history which could sweep up and "lose" within itself either state or individual.

Therefore, though the primary sense of Greek liberty refers almost exclusively to the freedom of the group, it was still of cardinal importance to the individual citizen. No doubt, on the ultimate level, so was Hegel's Idea of Freedom. But the freedom of the city was a personal concern for the Greek citizen, and the question of how to obtain it was for him a practical and immediate problem, not a metaphysical one. The question was not, "Which way does the course of real history lie?" but rather was, "How can I, in my life, be free if my city and its life are not?" If his city was in bondage, then he could serve, not her, but only a foreign master. And if he could not serve her, he could not fulfill his own moral needs. Participation would become an empty, purposeless activity. The freedom of the city was prerequisite not to the fulfillment of history but to the achievement of individual moral life.

The logic of this Greek argument for freedom of the city is ironclad. So long as participation in the local community continues as a moral vocation for men, this positive and communal sense of liberty will remain an important attribute of the meaning of citizenship, despite, or even because of, the individualism inherent in the Periclean contribution. "Home rule" remains, even until today, a goal and an ideal both for cities and for their citizens.

In the Greek tradition, home rule for the city also implied something definite in the way of real personal freedom for the citizens. The theory behind the Greek free city could not permit the absolute direction of all from a single center of authority, such as is characteristic of modern totalitarian and collectivistic philosophies. The heart of that theory was "participation" by and for individuals. There can be no genuine and cooperative participation by individuals unless they are free in some measure. To fulfill its role of making men good, the state must be free not only externally but internally as well. Pericles (Thucydides) was only stating an obvious precondition of the vitality of Athenian democracy when he claimed for his city that

. . . we are called a democracy, for the administration is in the hands of the many and not of the few. But while the law secures equal justice to all alike in their private disputes, the claim of excellence is also recognized; and when a citizen is in a way distinguished, he is preferred to the public service, not as a matter of privilege, but as the reward of merit. Neither is poverty a bar, but a man may benefit his country whatever be the obscurity of his condition. There is no exclusiveness in our public life, and in our private intercourse we are not suspicious of one another, nor angry with our neighbour if he does what he likes; we do not put on sour looks at him which, though harmless, are not pleasant.[15]

The notion of "The Free City" constitutes only half of the Periclean Ideal. Expression of the whole can only be given by the phrase "The Free Citizen in his Free City."

Both must be free, both alive and growing before we can conjure up the image of that vibrant communal life for which Athens has been for so long the symbol.

Nevertheless, even though the charge of Hegelianism is simply irrelevant, doubts persist for the modern mind about the Periclean notion of liberty. We, who now have the notion of individual will, can perhaps excuse the Greek philosophers for talking so much about *making* men good on the superior grounds that they, after all, did not know any better. We can simply pretend that if we were in charge of an Athens we would be careful to limit the activities of the state to establishing conditions within which men could make *themselves* good. But it is both fair and pertinent to ask of the Greeks (and all who adopt their ideal), "Good at what?" What are the citizens, in terms of this ideal, to be allowed to do? The justification of a grant of liberty must be by reference to the purposes which the grant is supposed to allow men to achieve. Since the Greeks defined citizenship solely in terms of participation, since man, in the days of Pericles, was regarded as being simply a social animal, all interest which men might have became public interests. (No wonder they defined politics to include so much we think nonpolitical.) Therefore, for the Greeks, personal liberty could only be the liberty to participate in the "politics" of their community, and justification of individual grants of liberty could only be made by showing that each grant in some way increased the vitality and prosperity of the community. Freedom then is, as Robert Frost has in fact only recently defined it, "feeling easy in your harness." [16]

Burns puts very neatly the difference between this aspect of Greek liberty and ours when he argues that for the Greeks liberty meant the possibility of a direct individual share in public activities; to us it more usually means the possibility of avoiding the political absorption of the individual.[17]

The consequences of this difference are many. The most obvious is that the Greeks would insist upon vastly increasing both the rights and the practice of political participation which we possess. Provincialism would be encouraged, local governments vitalized, and the powers of central governments correspondingly reduced. At the same time, they would be unable to understand and probably would abolish many of our so-called private rights (i.e., rights to privacy in the performance *and* justification of certain acts) of which the freedom of religion is only the most easily noted. But the definition and defense of liberty solely in public terms has at least two other consequences of serious import, both of which received dramatic illumination in the history of Athens.

The first of these is that the granting of liberty for public purposes alone precludes, obviously, the granting of it for private purposes. The Athenians were individualists; the perfection which they sought was the perfection of men. But their individualism was, from our point of view, of a singularly collectivistic nature. By insisting that individual salvation was to be found only in the group, the individual could be understood as being of value only in social terms, only as a member of the group. The Greeks were incapable of conceiving the individual as being valuable in himself, of being a unique entity burdened with problems primarily his own. They could not imagine themselves morally obligated to respect him and assist him even though his salvation might well contribute absolutely nothing to the happiness and salvation of the group. The criteria by which they judged their city were the quality and quantity of the good citizens it produced. Which individuals were to be so produced, which were to be left out, and the question of whether the results looked remarkably the same were matters of indifference so long as the standard of production remained high.

This is one consequence of defining the life of the citizen solely in terms of the life of his city. And if evidence is wanted of how far the Athenians were willing to go in this absence of concern for persons as persons, and of what this meant in terms of personal liberties, Zimmern provides it in a footnote on ostracism. He refers to

Plutarch's story of the countryman who wanted to . . . [ostracize] . . . Aristeides because he was tired of hearing him called the Just (Plut. *Arist.* 7). Athenians' acquiescence in the institution of ostracism shows how, as a matter of course, they put the city first and the individual nowhere. A man was ostracized for no offence whatsoever, but simply because a large proportion of his fellow-citizens thought he would be better out of the way. Nowadays such powers cannot be exercised even by schoolmasters.[18]

Beyond this consequence is another of such somber and profound dimensions as to be only properly described as theological. The requirements of the Greek tradition were that the city must be free and that citizens must be free in their service to her. Other than this there was, in the Periclean Ideal by itself, nothing. Except for pride in his city and in the quality of his service to her there was nothing by which the citizen could judge himself and, what was worse, nothing by which he could judge the performance and ambitions of his city. There might be old and inherited rules of good conduct, but if these were to be observed only because the city accepted them, then the city could as easily discard them in the search for immediate comforts.

When the vitality of the communal life is the only ideal, when the wants of the city become the only measure of righteousness, the city becomes a law unto itself. The end can only be self-destruction. This, surely, is the lesson and the tragedy which Thucydides set himself to describe in the *History*. The nobility of the Funeral Oration must be put beside the brutality of the Melian Dialogue. In the former, the Athenians are portrayed as reverent and honorable in terms of the old traditions; in the latter as mere seekers after the immediate, selfish ambitions of their city. City-state patriotism may well be the most lasting of the Greek contributions to our understanding of citizenship, but patriotism by itself is a poor guide to honor.

In sum, Athenian Citizenship presents to us initially something quite splendid. It is by no means unintelligible to us. We are, in fact, sympathetic to it and we can, and often do, transfer the picture it drew of itself long ago to our own times, most especially to our discussions of our home-ruling, self-governing local communities. We share the Greek pride in being able to participate, and subscribe to the doctrine that through participation full and satisfying lives may be lived. For us, as for the Greeks, the citizen and his community are bound in intimate relation not only by the very nature of the concept of citizenship but also by moral imperative. "The Free Citizen of the Free City" is a noble ideal; and it is also an enduring one.

At the same time, this ideal, unless greatly modified in implication and practical consequence, can be treacherous. There *is* something totalitarian in it, something anti-individual in our modern sense, which may condemn us to being free only to participate. There is hidden in it, too, a germ of self-conceit, that high, hard, and provincial pride which can disenfranchise the humble, set all citizens in a pattern of conformity, and exclude the stranger. And it can destroy souls.

The notion that "he who enjoys the right of sharing in deliberative or judicial office (for any period, fixed or un-fixed) attains thereby the status of citizen of his state," [19] together with the social values which sustain such a defini-tion, constitutes a part of the total amalgam which we have come to label citizenship. It accounts for the pride which the modern citizen feels in participating in the self-govern-ment of his community. The tradition has been passed down to us in a remarkably clear and direct manner. The self-governing cities dotted throughout the Alexandrian and Roman empires, the practice of the medieval city-states, all kept alive the tradition, though few of them ever at-tained the full measure of Athenian democracy. And Greek philosophy, a consistent staple of Western intellectual life, continued to teach the essential doctrines. The Western so-cial mind has never lacked the didactic example of the Greek *polis*

But, as a supposed complete definition of the modern concept of citizenship, the "public-office" definition from ancient Greece is notably deficient. It conveys very little of the spirit of the Bill of Rights, the universalistic demand by citizens for recognition as each worthy in himself alone. The Greek definition is not merely too institutional for this; it is too parochial. In the second place, it fails to de-scribe in our terms, or even to allow much opportunity to describe in our terms, the personal character of the modern citizen. The modern citizen is a restless agent, a man of energy, with problems, ambitions, and a vocation of his own. These concerns may be public or private in effect, but they are always personal because they are always *his*. For this, the Greek sense of personality is simply too weak.

B : THE HEBRAIC PATTERN

In the face of this, it is inevitable that we should turn to the other great source of modern culture, the Hebraic tradition, for further light on the nature of the modern democratic citizen. There is no denying the importance of the ancient Hebrews in the making of the modern Western mind, but it is extremely difficult to get agreement on what (and how) they contributed. The source of this difficulty lies in the character of the Hebrews themselves. In its techniques, the modern mind, especially the modern scholarly mind, is essentially Greek. It proceeds primarily through close analysis and reasoned argument. The philosopher-scientist is its ideal. The rationally ordered body of abstract principle applicable to proved fact is the hoped-for result.

The contrast to this of the Hebraic mind as represented in Biblical literature could not be sharper. The prime figure there is the prophet-narrator. The concern is not for knowledge, for truth about things in propositional form. The prophets did not, nor did they even attempt to, write philosophical treatises on metaphysics or ethics. Instead, to put it crudely, they told rather violent stories, listed commandments, and passed judgments.

As a result, the Greek-formed modern scholar finds the Hebrew literature not a little baffling. He knows it to be important—and all the textbook collections-of-selections now begin with generous excerpts from Deuteronomy and Matthew. But when the set questions are asked, "What for the Hebrews was the nature of the state, of man, of God?" or "What were for the Hebrews the basic principles of social ethics?" the answers are very imprecise. They are bound to be. The Hebrews never asked these questions and, therefore, never gave any answers to them. We ask them now and now must seek out answers never more than implied in a diverse collection of stories, parables, laws, and judgments for which the major "evidence" (in our modern sense) is usually merely the repeated statement "Thus saith the Lord."

The guess hazarded here is that the modern scholarly mind frequently is blind except to its own image. The Hebraic contribution to modern social theory, especially to the modern democratic conception of the citizen, is immense. This contribution can be usefully discussed under two heads: first, the vitality and uniqueness of the individual; and, second, the problem of loyalty and service. But the caution must be added that we must not suppose that the Hebraic contributions to modern notions of citizenship were made, under either of these heads, in the clear and direct manner characteristic of the Greek. In every case, the Hebraic contributions had to be first absorbed, and then cast into formal shape, by later contexts, of which the imperial Roman tradition, for example, was one of the most important. The modern notion of citizenship is a theoretical concept which has place and meaning only within a political theory or theories—and the Hebrews neither wrote nor had a political theory in this formal sense. As a consequence, a truly imaginative effort must be made if the Hebraic character of much that is in modern citizenship is to be given the appreciation it deserves.

Related to this difficulty in the way of discovering and appreciating the Hebraic origins of some of our modern social beliefs about citizenship is a problem of exposition. It is convenient to keep the present chapter primarily concerned with the origins of those aspects of modern citizenship which bind the individual to his community, and to reserve for the next chapter treatment of those conceptions which insist upon separating the citizen from his social context. But the Hebraic mind of which the Old Testament is the primary expression spawned both the notion of the vital and unique individual and the problem of loyalty and service. And what is worse, for expository purposes, it presented this notion and this problem not as separate conceptions but rather as part and parcel of a single and apparently indivisible attitude toward life. In the embryonic form in which they appear in the Old Testament, these two conceptions simply cannot be properly discussed separately. Yet in our day these two conceptions, as they presently appear, have been separated drastically. In his unique vitality, the individual now stands defiantly apart from his community; by the loyalty which he owes to his community, he now is bound to it. Much of the next chapter will be concerned with the process by which this historic separation was achieved. For the present chapter, these two conceptions must be considered in their undifferentiated form. The problem of loyalty and service is, then, the immediate concern, and the extensive discussion of Hebraic individuality, which perforce we must turn to next, is to be viewed in the first instance as contributing to an understanding of that problem. But the reader is asked to be prepared to recall this discussion of Hebraic individuality when we come, in the next chapter, to the discussion of the Hebraic contribution to the development of the first patterns of Western individualism.

Perhaps the most rapid way of fastening attention on the Hebraic origins of modern notions of individuality is to point out how seldom modern discussions of the problem of rights dwell at any length on the question of whether men actually will use the opportunities of freedom. There is, of course, ample denunciation of people who do not exercise their rights and much exhortation, but there is a singular lack of any immediate awareness that throughout much of our literature the activity potential of persons is simply assumed. They *will* act—the only questions being how and to what ends. Like Hobbes, we tend to "put for a general inclination of all mankind, a perpetual and restless desire of power after power, that ceaseth only in death." [20] But unlike Hobbes, we assume this perpetual activity in man not because of metaphysical convictions but because of an ethical bias. An era in which little is accomplished, in which life is merely lived day by day in a changeless and simple serenity would be, for us, very nearly a dead age, a worthless and utterly uninteresting passing up of obvious opportunities to be alive and doing. Our only pressing problem would seem to be to set men free, to release the pent-up creative energies which we know to be in them.

I do not decry this ethical bias in any way, but I would suggest that the origins of it cannot be found in any Greek conception of the ideal state. Rather the origins of it are to be discovered in the propensity of the writers of Hebraic literature—a literature which has lain on tens of thousands more bedside tables than has Plato's *Republic*—to see man as a soul, a will, a power active in history. There are two aspects of this, one the attitude toward the energy and activity of the individual himself and the other the stress laid upon the space-time context of history within which the action takes place. For purposes of comparison, we need only remember from time to time how little either is emphasized by the Greeks, particularly by their philosophers.

The Hebraic attitude toward the individual in himself is revealed in the first instance by the manner in which the Hebrews set about trying to discuss and solve their problems. For the Greeks, and probably also for many of us today, man's primary identifying characteristic was the possession of reason, and his most characteristic activity was thinking. But, for the Hebrew, thinking was not the solving of abstract problems. Rather, thinking was for him the activity of grasping on to a totality and making it thereby something possessed. In Hebrew there is no word which quite corresponds to our verb "to think." There are words which mean "to remember," "to make present," "to investigate," and the like. But none of these convey the analysis and arrangement of ideas. The Hebrew thinker was not concerned to relate ideas one to another. He was concerned to relate ideas to himself and to be prompted by that experience, by that activity, to embark on new experience, on new activity.[21]

When we follow Greek thinkers, we tend to assume "thinking" to be a faculty, a capacity to *perceive* that this or that is true or exists. There is an unconscious tendency to transfer the static quality of perception to that which is perceived, to arrest the object of thought while inspecting to see if it is mortal or adds up to 180°. In contrast, for the Hebrew thinkers (and it is misleading even to call them that), thinking was not a faculty, not a capacity but an activity. It was an activity by which the soul related itself to, or directed itself toward, or absorbed into itself some object or idea, god or commandment.

Because the stress was laid on the activity of relation to, rather than on analysis of, the object, the Hebrews neither invented nor employed all those abstract distinctions which we have come to recognize as the stock in trade of the philosophically inclined; distinctions between body and soul, between material and immaterial, between the natural and the supernatural, between, in a single ethical act, the intent, the desire, the will, the act itself, and the consequences. There has been much controversy over the years about whether the Hebrews, for example, believed in a supernatural God, or, for a further example, in immortality. Most of such controversy has been simply beside the point. The Hebrews neither believed nor disbelieved in a *supernatural* God. God was a present something who acted in the present, and beyond that the Hebrews did not pursue the matter. The question of immortality is also, so far as the Hebrews are concerned, very nearly irrelevant. To debate this question intelligently one must be prepared to distinguish between that part of the self that dies, the body, and that part, the soul, which is supposed, or not, to live on after death. Even those who deny the possibility of immortality must make use of the distinction between these two, if only to deny the existence of any reality corresponding to the soul. But the Hebrews, though they had separate words for body, soul, heart, and spirit, distinguished between them only in the vaguest way. In most cases, the words were easily interchangeable. The closest the Hebrews came to a doctrine of immortality was in connection with the subject of resurrection, but on this their attitude, so far as modern scholarship can determine, was literal simplicity. The references to it in the latter part of the Old Testament and throughout the New are not, apparently, to be fundamentally distinguished from the references, in the earliest books, to ghosts and spirits, dead persons who were in some mysterious way half alive. Resurrection was simply the reactivation of the composite body-soul which previously had been dead, i.e., had stopped acting.

It is the notion of man as a complete, undifferentiated totality which we must recapture first if we are to grasp the Hebrew attitude toward man. It is not enough for us, who do make the distinction between body and soul, simply to add the two together. The Hebrews did not add pieces together. Man was man, the whole man, and all that was of him was the man himself. The Hebraic word for soul is *nephesh,* but *nephesh* served to designate far more than even body plus soul as we understand those words. The soul of a man was the totality of his character, appearance, and experience: his manner of acting, the sound of his voice, the more or less hairy quality of his skin, his smell, all that he had done, all that had ever happened to him, all that belonged to him, his clothes, his family, his house. All of these taken together and grasped in their uniqueness constituted the soul, the man.[22]

This insistence on viewing things always as undifferentiable totalities can easily, and in the Hebraic tradition, certainly did, produce, as we shall be noting in a moment, an overpowering sense of community, of the oneness of the tribe or nation. But the point that should be stressed here is that this attitude, on the level of individuals, produces absolutely the reverse effect. If the mental equipment for differentiation in abstract terms is available, then it becomes only too easy to shear off from you and me, our fathers, wives, children, and neighbors, all those peculiarities of individuality such as manner of dress, lilt of speech, degree of intelligence, and so on, and leave us all in the impersonal, naked sameness of the one category: human beings. But this the Hebrew could not do. When he looked at a man, he saw *a* man, a unique being who was all that he ever had been, all that he now was, wore, had, loved, *lived,* all that he ever would be. No wonder that the Hebrew cherished so much his name, for his name was the one constant around which clustered all the variety of his life and which represented the whole of his unique totality of experience. Men, of course, could be bound into groups by common covenant or common blood. But when *a* Tom and *a* Dick and *a* Harry are gathered together, you cannot, with a Hebraic attitude, refer easily to "any Tom, Dick, or Harry." You can only speak of "Tom, the son of . . . ,

Dick, who slew . . . , and Harry, the man who was . . ."

It may be true, as a kind of psychosociological general-ization, that peoples who do not (or *will* not) differentiate philosophically, allow history to differentiate for them. But whether this is true as a generalization or not, it seems, certainly, to be applicable to the Hebraic approach of "I am what I have become, you are what you have become and *there* is the difference between us." And this throws into focus the other major characteristic of the Hebraic attitude toward man: the emphasis on the story and, therefore, on the activity of individuals.

But the Hebrews were not fascinated merely by motion in activity. What attracted their lively curiosity was always the source of the activity. The primary question was always "Who did it and why?" A good deal of exaggeration and even inaccuracy in the answer to questions about what happened could be tolerated so long as the agents involved in the action were properly identified. A plague or a pes-tilence, a whirlwind or an earthquake, "a little cloud out of the sea, like a man's hand" [23] were fit subjects for intense interest but largely because any of them might be under-stood as signs of the presence and activity of Jehovah, the Lord God. Yahweh is great because these are great things which He has done. Much the same kind of measure is applied to men. They are great in so far as they can ac-complish. Greatness is not merely physical strength, though much prominence is often given to feats of strength. But the major kind of strength noted in Biblical literature is what we would call, perhaps, strength of character. The hero-leader is the man who proves again and again that he has such strength of will that he can force it to enter into the wills of others and bend them all in one common direc-tion. This description is somewhat inaccurate because the Hebrews had no separate word for our term "will." When referring to volition, they used the same word, *nephesh,* as for soul, or else one of its equivalents, heart or spirit. The explanation in part is that, since they always conceived of man whole, it would have been inappropriate as well as impossible to conceive of the will as a separate faculty of the soul. But the complete explanation must refer also to the fact that for the Hebrews the concept is never of man, or even of man whole but always of the whole man alive. The soul is not a thing; it is a force; it is a being in directed motion. The concept is of man vital and of death as man unvital, for ". . . at death, man is like water which has been spilt upon the ground and cannot be gathered up."[24] When King David was near death, the narrator did not find it sufficient to say that he "was old and stricken in years." He goes on to prove that vitality is gone by relating explicitly how the king is now incapable of performing the male act.[25]

The only context within which man as thus understood can be placed is the time-space context of history. Only in history can a man acquire that wealth of individual associations, experiences, habits, and possessions which will mark him off forever as unique and unrepeatable. Only history can supply these innumerable details in myriad combinations. And only history can provide the stage upon which these unique beings can expend their energies, pursue their purposes, and attain their goals. The Hebraic man is inevitably and pre-eminently a historic figure, a creature both of and in his time and place.

This is the source and the strength of the Hebraic sense of personality. For the writers of the Testaments, God was a person. His name was Yahweh.[26] He was both Lord of History and an actor in history, who repeatedly made His presence felt in the affairs of men and in the movements of nature. And men were persons, each with vitality, strengths, and weaknesses, each with problems, ambitions, and fears. There is nothing in the Hebraic mind to compare with that Greek ideal, timeless and pure, order without flaw within which supremely rational men could slough off the cares, flesh, and dust of this life to contemplate the better an eternal Truth. The Hebrews did not turn their backs on history; they faced history. They lived their lives, as men must, in this life, in this place, in this time: their literature is filled with "do's" and "don'ts" to direct and restrain the errant energies of men in daily life. By paradigm and parable, they have been teaching and consoling common folk, ordinary, unimportant *persons,* ever since.

The Hebraic tradition did more than define men as unique and vital. It also defined, or better, assumed the outlines of, a problem in the life of each man the demands of which overrode in importance all other needs. This was the problem of loyalty. It was not a question of "shall I be loyal?" Man, as soul, as vital force, would to that extent devote his energies to the service of some thing or god in some way or another. This was simply assumed. The only explicit problem was "To what or to whom shall I be loyal?" or, "For whom shall I expend my energies?"

This is the obvious way to state the question and it is the form in which most of the discussion of it in the Bible is presented. The great contest between the prophet Elijah and Jezebel, the alien wife of King Ahab, which reached its climax in the test to burn bullocks, was essentially a dispute over whether the God of Abraham, Isaac, and Jacob should continue to receive the loyalty of Israel or whether, as Jezebel wished, loyalty should be transferred to the god she had "brought with her" from her native land. The destruction by Moses of the Golden Calf and the denunciation by the eighth-century prophet Amos of the inhabitants of the Northern Kingdom are both motivated by the same charge: the children of Israel have, for a traditional object of loyalty, substituted another.

. . . thou shalt worship no other god: for the Lord whose name is Jealous, is a jealous God: Lest thou make a covenant with the inhabitants of the land, and they go a whoring after their gods . . .[27]

But the question "To whom shall I be loyal?" can be stated in another way which, though more awkward and less sharp, is yet more accurate and more descriptive of all that was involved: "In what *community* am I to find common vocation?" This is a more accurate statement of the Hebraic intention because it eliminates ambiguity. It is quite possible that I should dedicate myself to obey a rule of conduct, abstract and impersonal. The Hebrews, of course, pledged themselves to obey the Law but only because and in so far as that Law was received as the expression of God. The loyalty which they assumed was for them necessarily a loyalty of a servant to a master. The act of loyalty was the surrendering of the direction of the will, as we would call it, to some other, presumably higher, will. Again, the sense of personality is essential. Only a person can command, only a person can obey. The taking on of a vocation to obey a master presupposed, in the Hebraic mind, the establishment of a communal relationship between persons. The servant must pledge obedience, but also the master must promise to command. The two were bound to live together so long as their common covenant continued.

At the same time that the Hebrews assumed, for the problem of loyalty, what might be termed a vertical community between master and servant, they as easily assumed a horizontal community between the many servants all bound to the same master. They did not ignore the numerous mundane ties which bind men in community, ties of common language, common history, and, above all in the Hebraic tradition, common kinsmanship. But they capped these ties with the notions of one God for all, and, more important, consciously understood and expressed their unity in terms of it. This was particularly important, no doubt, in the periods both before and after the time of their political independence in Palestine, but throughout their history, at least in their own understanding, what made them finally *one* tribe, one nation was the fact of their common loyalty. They were one because they had one common vocation, obedience to the God, Yahweh, with Whom they had covenanted.

This approach to the community by the Hebraic mind was reinforced by certain of its own characteristics which we have already had occasion to notice. The willingness to view an individual man's soul as extending throughout all that was associated with him created in turn a willingness to equate the man with his tribe. This is particularly pronounced in the cases of men who ruled and led their peoples. Scholars often have exceptional difficulty, especially in the early books of the Old Testament, in determining whether a personal name such as Benjamin refers to a single individual or to the whole tribe of whom Benjamin was the "father." The propensity to view anything that "acted" as, at one and the same time, a totality and a personality translated this willingness into a positive eagerness. To be sure, the notion of common kinsmanship received in the Hebrew tradition quite extraordinary emphasis and found expression in the frequency with which the common ancestry is traced back to the one father, Abraham. But this was never allowed to conceal or belittle the idea that the people of Israel had evolved a common soul. That soul, or as we, in almost inevitable imitation of Rousseau, would call it, that "General Will," had acted as a single entity in coming out of Egypt, in conquering the Canaanites, in warring with the Philistines, above all in covenanting with Yahweh. This was not mere literary personification. *Nephesh*, soul, rarely occurs in the plural in Hebraic literature[28] simply because the Hebrews just assumed that a group of individual souls acting together had a single soul, that is, a single force and direction for their common activity. When they met together to discuss their problems they did not come, as do modern parliaments, to argue the merits of various proposals and decide by majority vote. They met to establish a psychic community among men sitting together. They met when there was disunity, when there were divergent opinions about what ought to be done. No doubt, on such occasions, there was lively debate and much dispute. But the characteristic manner of arriving at a decision, for restoring unity, was for one man, by the vigor of his speech and the force of his personality, to bend to his the wills of all those assembled. In this way they again became of one heart, again became one nation having but one will.[29]

All of these points about the community—that it was a community of persons, that they found their oneness in their common vocation, that the resultant totality was *a* totality supposed, even, to have a common soul or will—found expression in the concept of the covenant. We are apt to think that for the Hebrews there was only the one covenant, the Covenant with Yahweh made at Sinai. We tend to forget that this was, in a sense, a covenant renewed and that it was to be renewed again and again and even revised. And we tend to be quite unaware that the covenant was a constant device by which the Hebrews sought to stabilize their relationships, one man with his neighbor, his creditor, his king, and the whole tribe with other tribes with whom it might have occasion to deal from time to time. But the Covenant of Sinai was the crucial covenant, and from it we can catch something of the spirit of the Hebraic sense of community which no mere analysis of its parts can provide. The writers of the Old Testament never set out the terms of that Covenant in the legalistic form one expects from the seventeenth-century social contractarians of our own era. But the ritual by which it was consummated and which is described is enlightening.

And Moses wrote all the words of the Lord, and rose up early in the morning, and builded an altar under the hill, and twelve pillars, according to the twelve tribes of Israel. And he sent young men of the children of Israel, which offered burnt offerings, and sacrificed peace offerings of oxen unto the Lord. And Moses took half of the blood, and put it in basons; and half of the blood he sprinkled on the altar. And he took the book of the covenant, and read in the audience of the people: and they said, All that the Lord hath said will we do, and be obedient. And Moses took the blood, and sprinkled it on the people, and said, Behold the blood of the covenant, which the Lord hath made with you concerning all these words.[30]

Scholarly comment on this runs as follows:

The meaning of this ritual is not far to seek. The blood is the life [Lev. 17:11, 14], the vital essence. Two parties, at present independent one of another, are to be united in a single whole, and, to secure the desired union, a third party is introduced. Its life is taken from it and made available for the other two. Both come under it, both are included in it, the same vital essence now covers and embraces the two. They are thus no longer independent entities, they are one, finding their unity with each other in their unity with that third party whose blood now covers them both. Till this point is reached, however near they might have brought one to another, they are merely contiguous; now they are continuous, and form parts of a single indivisible whole. We might almost say that now Yahweh is Himself included in the term Israel; henceforward it will connote not merely human community, but one of which He is a member.[31]

Thus is the community born, renewed, and, most important, remembered. The children of Israel become the chosen people not because they are better or, for that matter, worse than others. It was long the view that other people and other places would appropriately have other gods to serve. But the Hebrews had been chosen by *their* God, Yahweh, and, in turn, they had acknowledged Him as theirs. It was this mutual choice which made them "chosen," which made them a people and which placed upon them an enduring burden of rights and duties, of service. By the act of covenant they achieved a common vocation, a unity of service, a common soul. Let them fail in the performance of their obligations, and their bonds would collapse, their unity would weaken, and the vigor would run out of their soul. Let them remember their Covenant and they would endure as long as the God with Whom and to Whom they had pledged—which is forever.

There is much in this that is naïve and primitive. Experts in comparative religion assure us that many of the features of early Hebrew religious life are common to the religious practices of primitive peoples throughout history. From the point of view of these experts, Hebrew religion is hardly unique. But, as has been argued earlier, it is unique for us of the West: largely because of the accident, historically speaking, that literary records of this particular religion were kept and then assiduously preserved and handed down to us in revered form, its "primitive notions" have become part and parcel of our life today. They affect and, in some instances, largely determine not only much of our present-day religious life but also much of our philosophy, of our social ethics, of our politics, of our very way of understanding ourselves and our relations to each other. The Hebraic literature has been preached for so long and to so many of us that this can hardly be supposed otherwise.

Of all these effects the ones which are of most concern here are those which have contributed to the vast array of presuppositions which we make about the individual and his place in and relations to his community. Certainly the notion of each individual as historically unique and vital is a cardinal portion of the modern sense of individualism. Only through the persistence of this notion could intractable resistance be offered to the rationalistic and universalistic tendencies to drop men impersonally into categories of "workers," "juvenile delinquents," or, to use a stronger example, "cannon fodder." Though we often employ categories of this sort, we are as yet incapable of applying them with consistent vigor. As soon as we get close to them, they begin to evaporate: we see inside them too many unique and vital and interesting individuals. Each man is a case, and our law, at least, still strives to test each case on its merits. Each man is a personality, a soul, and how he controls and directs the energy thereof is a matter of pressing interest to him and to us all.

But however much we stress this individualistic aspect of the Hebraic tradition, it must be admitted that within that tradition this aspect is but the germ of what is to come. Until the Hebraic mind is set in other and contrasting contexts—until, in fact, the nation that was Israel is broken up and its culture translated into other circumstances—this germ remains only a germ. Within the purely Hebraic, the individual is so closely bound up in his community that his undoubted personality never became truly "personal," private.

On the other hand, the Hebraic individual, regarded in community with his fellows and his god, provides us with something much more directly related to present-day experience. This concept, too, had to wait generations before being fully developed, but implicit in the Hebraic problem of communal loyalty and service was a definition of the community both altogether different from the Greek and altogether familiar to us. By implication, the Hebraic community was what we would now call organic. So too was the Greek: both were "wholes" rather than "aggregates"; both achieved their unity from having imposed on the parts an idea, a way and purpose for the communal life. But in the difference between the respective purposes lay, as result, a wholesale difference between the characters of the corresponding communities. The purpose of the Greek community was to make men good, and the individual citizen established himself as a member of it by finding the niche appropriate to his talents, as philosopher-king or warrior or artisan. In that niche he fitted as a contributing member to the self-sufficiency and order of the city. His merits as a citizen were measured by the quality of his contribution. In contrast, the Hebraic community existed to keep the Covenant with Yahweh. Rather than self-sufficiency of order, it had a "destiny" to "meet" and that destiny was, in a sense, exterior to itself. The community had a mission in history. The citizen, for such he would ultimately be called, was measured not in terms of his abilities and what they produced but in terms of his willingness to accept the communal mission as his personal vocation. In the Hebraic community, at least by implication, the citizen became and remained truly a member only by proving himself a *loyal* citizen. All other qualifications were matters of indifference when compared to this one.

The full development to historical prominence of the

loyal or patriotic citizen is, of course, a comparatively recent matter. It is bound up with the emergence in our own era of democratic nationalism. But if we bear in mind the example of the Hebraic community where the demand for loyalty was not only a primary demand but also was very nearly the only demand the community made upon individuals, we can see more clearly the far-reaching ramifications of this aspect of citizenship than we would if we studied only the present and thoroughly complicated situation. In the Hebraic community we can see without distraction that the communal demand for loyalty from individuals put a premium on the virtue of *being* loyal, on the *activity* of rightfully directing the energies of the soul. And, further, that virtue does not merely consist in the activity as such. It consists in being actively loyal *to* the accepted, the community-adopted god. "Disloyalty" is not "*un*loyalty"; wrong willing is not to be *un*willing. The sin is idolatry, loyalty to the wrong god, loyalty to some object other than that accepted as orthodox. The sin is wrong choosing and wrong serving, and it is neither indolence nor inefficiency, bureaucratic or otherwise.

How terribly and awfully familiar have these phrases become: "disloyal," "unreliable," "security-risk." Among the anxieties of the modern world, right loyalty has become the first and, also, very nearly the last criterion for determining who should be citizens. It is true that in law *jus sanguinis* and *jus soli* are the most usual formulas. It is true that we ask for deeds, empirically verifiable facts, not words. It is true that we do not actually charge our suspected civil servants with idolatry. But all this is due to the difficulty of proving idolatry: there are no means by which to measure the existence of a man's soul, much less its deviation from the right direction. Yet, behind all our loyalty tests, there can be no doubt that it is the wrong-god-serving activity that we fear, that the traitor must be hanged for his apostasy, not for his crime. We call for deeds, but the first deed required is to swear a great oath.

All this is of the citizen and his loyalty. The ramifications of the Hebraic concepts on the definition of the community are equally strange and no less terrifying. They begin simply enough. Loyalty is now seen to be the common bond. Each citizen is now understood to share with the rest the same experience of being loyal to an identical object. Each can therefore *trust* the rest, and mutual trust is emphasized as the absolute prerequisite to confident communal life. This trust is that all will act in conformity with the common interest which has become, through the loyalty of each, the overriding private interest of each.

But this is only the beginning. We have seen how in the Hebraic tradition to be loyal was to surrender the direction of the will to some other, presumably higher, will. Only by personification of the object of loyalty as well as of the subject could obedience be meaningfully rendered. That which I love, lives—whatever it may be. And we have also seen how for the Hebrews by the act of covenant they became one with Yahweh and He one with them; how, in effect, the Living God came to live in the community. Here, in embryo, is the most awful of modern social inventions, the semidivine nation-state which *lives* in history. Granted that it was a long time coming to its modern form. Granted, too, that the factors determining its evolution were many and diverse. But the concepts in terms of which it could be recognized and then proclaimed and extolled were long available. With the breakup of the unity of medieval Europe and the particularization of the national communities, it was easy, however idolatrous, for a philosopher to claim that *his* nation was the march of God in history.

Of course, some philosophers, being more speculative

than the simple-minded Hebrews, could abstract out individual will as a faculty of individual soul and could thereby stress, if they so chose, the individuality of each grant of loyalty to the state. They could insist on the necessity of individual consent. But once consent has been given, once loyalty has been declared, what then? Is partial surrender of the direction of will either possible or likely to be approved? Is a promise to be *in*completely obedient likely to satisfy an ambitious god, to say nothing of a jealous one? Of course, again, other philosophers could insist that the existence of a national, suprapersonal will was only a morally necessary postulation. If the individual is to obey some will other than his own, if, in other words, he is to have the opportunity to be unselfish, a communal will must be postulated. Its postulation is a necessary ingredient in our moral experience, but its existence is only intellectual. Neat but *very* intellectual. Ordinary men are as simple-minded as anyone ever supposed the Hebrews to be. They will not catch, nor certainly act upon, a distinction between existences that are real and those that are only intellectual. What the philosopher says is a postulation they will believe is truly there, if they feel at all what the philosopher thinks to be a necessity. Once the citizen is defined in terms of loyalty and to the degree that he is, the anthropomorphization of the state, more or less articulated, follows as a practical inevitability. Once the citizen is defined in terms of loyalty and to the degree that he is, citizenship, ugly as this may sound to the modern democrat, will come to mean absolute conformity to the will of the living state. It matters not at all if the organization of the state is "democratic" or "dictatorial," nor if the governing class is the few best or the mediocre mass; once the citizen is *merely* loyal he must be *wholly* subservient.[32] This is not only the logically inescapable consequence. This is the practically and humanly necessary response to any state or situation thus viewed and understood.

The Greek and the Hebraic traditions, then, are the sources of two of the components of the modern concept of citizenship. The two parts are very different, as different as the two cultures which generated them. They are different both in themselves and in their implications. In one, the Greek, the emphasis is, we have suggested, philosophical: the role of the citizen must be *understood*, his function defined as a part of a conceptualized whole. It is a role which allows for considerable independence of performance, but yet it will have meaning and justification only as it is related to the whole of the drama of civic life. In the other, the Hebraic, the emphasis is correspondingly historical: the "citizen," the member of the Hebraic tribe, must *become* a member of a living community. The act of becoming, the act by which and in which the community of members was created, must be celebrated and remembered, for it is in the historicity of that act, not in any conceptualization of the community or its purpose, that the individual receives his rights, duties, and identity. In the city-state, the citizen is proud to occupy a place, respected and powerful, in the constitutionalized structure of his community; in the Hebrew tribe, the "citizen" shares the subservience imposed by the life of a common dedication. In the first, the primary virtue is active and appropriate participation; in the second, it is loyalty to the common mission.

Different as these two conceptions are, there is yet one great similarity between them. In both, the citizen is preeminently a member, a part, of importance only when *in* the group. Cut off or cast out of it, he is nothing, an outlander, a wanderer, a disinherited, hardly a man at all.

Furthermore, in both the Greek and Hebraic traditions, the community within which the individual had to find himself and his place was small. In Greece, the citizenship ideal was essentially urban; in Palestine, though the geography was more dispersed and the economy more mixed, the political organization remained essentially tribal.

These communities can also be called small in a looser and in a cultural sense. They were, when at the height of what might be called their pristine evolution, isolated, self-contained, and self-sufficient. It is true, of course, that in pre-fourth-century Greece, there was a measure of Pan-hellenic feeling; the common scorn for the "barbarian" non-Greek, the general influence of such things as the Delphic Oracle, to say nothing of the similarities of language and political and social organization, are all pointed to as revealing the early presence of a widely shared sense of common race. But these are better thought of as foreshadowings of a cosmopolitanism to come. For the early Greeks, the differences between the cities were more significant than all the similarities. Athens did not share the fullness of her life or her philosophy with all the world until after her dreams of empire had been shattered. The case of Palestine is even more clear-cut. Yahweh was the God of Israel, and the notion that out of Palestine could come a light for the Gentiles was a late development. Before the fall of Jerusalem there are few, and before the eighth century very few if any, hints of that monotheism which was an essential preliminary to the development from the early Hebraic beliefs of a religion for which universal truth and application could be claimed. The citizens of both early Greece and early Israel had to find the full meaning of their lives from within the narrow limits of the tiny communities into which they had been born. For this purpose the ideals of free participation and of loyal service, each within its own narrow circumstances, were very nearly sufficient. But when the circumstances changed, when isolation and smallness were lost, these ideals were found to be no longer enough.

III

THE CHRISTIAN-ROMAN PATTERN:

INDIVIDUALISM

PRIVATE CITIZEN AND
CITIZEN OF THE WORLD

The third ingredient of modern citizenship, which suggests men indignantly defensive about themselves and their privacy, can be viewed as one of the many products of the general process by which the Greek and Hebraic cultures were shaken out of their early isolation. These cultures gradually were freed to drift, combine, and grow throughout the civilized world. The process was long and complicated, and we must attempt to see at least enough of it to be able to pick out the development within it of something very new to the ancient world, the development of a sense of individualism.

The process by which the Greek and Hebrew communities lost the purity and simplicity of isolation can be most

83

briefly described by dividing it into two broad stages. The first was the period during which these early communities were forced to give up their political status as independent communities. The actual submissions in the two cases occurred at very different times but both took place in, very roughly, the same manner and with comparable effects. Both cultures, more or less as complete wholes, were caught up and swept out of their former isolation and into the new context of the emerging cosmopolitan empires.

The second broad stage of the process came later. It occurred when Rome absorbed into its own cultural mold, a mold of deliberately imperial and universal design, the traditions of these two more ancient cultures, gradually imposed upon them its own imprint, and, just as gradually, sought to combine them into one restless synthesis. That synthesis would ever be restless, never complete nor stable. There was serious contradiction in the very attempt at synthesis, for it was an attempt to combine and universalize philosophies and attitudes which, originally, not only were thoroughly insular, but also were only clearly meaningful within the neighborhood context of the local communities which germinated them. And the contrasts between the two main parts of the attempted mixture, between the rationalistic Greek and the voluntarist Hebraic, were (and still continue to be) so great as to make a really comfortable blending of them impossible. One notable consequence of the synthesis being, therefore, inevitably incomplete was its very restlessness, a restlessness which has given rise to that perpetual and anxious seeking after new solutions and that ancient longing for half-remembered, never recoverable, serenity of mind which have characterized the Western European mind ever since. Another consequence was that the old Greek and Hebraic ideas, never being completely absorbed into either each other or something new, retained a measure of their independent identities with much of their original meanings and associations.

But the synthesis was attempted. It has been and is being attempted repeatedly. Its incompleteness constitutes a standing and compulsive challenge to the ingenuities of the Western mind. The long history of these attempts and the fact that they all, in their essentials, are very similar, have created a distinctive group of ideas and attitudes for Western man. These are neither purely Greek nor Hebraic, though, considering the nature of their birth, there is much of both to be seen in them. On the contrary, they are Roman, or, to be more accurate and more inclusive, Christian-Roman, for the work of Augustine is more characteristic of them than is the work of Augustus. They are Roman because it was within the imperial Roman context that the first rigorous attempt at synthesis was made. They are Christian because it was Christianity which carried forward Rome's hunger for the universally true and the monolithically stable, Rome's demand for the impossible synthesis.

The development of a philosophy of individualism within the process which brought the Greek and Hebraic cultures into the central stream of Western development can be seen as including four fairly distinct steps. The first of these steps was taken in both Greece and Israel when events forced a genuine and perceptible loosening of the ties which for so long had bound the individual wholly within his local community. The second step followed closely on the first: the individual, thrown more and more on his own resources, developed for himself an intense and utterly personal "problem" or mission. Various Greek philosophers responded to the need to orient man's outlook in terms of the personal. But it was the Hebrews who most dramatically responded to this need and who contributed the definition of man's private occupation[1] which has most endured in the history of the West. The third step was taken within the context of the Roman Empire. The Romans, for their own imperial purposes and as instructed by the Greek philosophers, created a structure of institutions and ideas for their citizenship which constituted a pattern of individualism in everything except dynamic content. The fourth and final step was the work of the Christianized subjects of the Empire who, in the general attempt to synthesize the Greek and Hebraic cultures, succeeded quite remarkably in the specific task of imbedding the Hebraic definition of man's private occupation within the pattern established by the Roman definition of citizenship. The result was Western individualism after a pattern which has persisted down to the present day.

It would be wrong to view these steps toward individualism as rigidly and simply successive, and it will be difficult, in discussing them, to maintain clear separation between them. But, if we attempt to discuss each of them one by one, we can see more clearly the development in the ancient world of not only a sense, a feeling, of individualism, but also of a conceptualization and reasonably systematic justification for it in a form which could be and was widely accepted and which could be and was made to become at least a part of the orthodox philosophy of life.

A

The first of these steps, that by which the individual was pried loose from the too intimate life of the neighborhood community, was a direct consequence of the shattering loss of political independence by the early Greek and Hebraic communities. In each case, the individual was forced to adapt his outlook to the fact that his community's continued vitality now depended on political factors and cultural conditions outside its own immediate ken and control. To the degree that he acknowledged the relative permanence of the new conditions, he was forced inward to a greater self-reliance and also, outward, toward a greater recognition and acceptance of values and peoples other than his own. Both ways pointed to a lessening of dependence on neighborhood community for definition of the meaning and purpose of his life.

How this happened in Hebraic history is easily seen. The two little Palestinian kingdoms were finally crushed by the sheer weight and ambitions of their powerful neighbors. One can only marvel that they had survived independent for so long, surrounded as they had been by such jealous and competing powers as Egypt, Assyria, and Babylon. Certainly the great prophets of the eighth century, Amos, Hosea, and Isaiah, were acutely conscious of Palestine's geographically focal position and therefore, also, of the probability of doom. And the crushing blows did finally descend. But of almost greater significance was the fact that, as a result of the national disasters and defeats, a portion of the population, important more in terms of status than in numbers, was taken off to live in exile in the land of the conquerors. The Exile was much more than a national humiliation, a tragedy to be remembered and the end of an epoch. It was also a turning point in the development of the Hebraic religion. The exiles were forced, by the harsh alternatives of either making the necessary adjustments or abandoning altogether the sense of the historic community, to adapt their Yahwehist religion to their new condition. No longer could they turn to their god as simply a god of nation and place. They could not turn to him as the god of the Jews in Israel. They had to turn to him, if they would turn to him still, as the god of Jews where-ever they individually might be and whatever their individual condition. This marked, however tentatively, the beginning in the Hebraic tradition of *personal* religion.

These beginnings of a personal element in Hebraic religion were not, especially as their immediate cause had been so clearly anticipated, without precursors. The most ancient of these and the one which, more than any other aspect of the Hebraic tradition, was to have the most lasting impact on the evolution of later social theory, was the fact that Hebraic religion had been, from the time of its earliest records, distinctive for its record of moral protest by individuals against the prevailing social order. Certainly there existed in Hebraic religion the narrow, prudential, the almost magical elements, and these were long chiefly emphasized. They are obvious in many of the ritual prescriptions and even crop up in the commandments: "Honour thy father and thy mother: that [i.e., *in order that*] thy days may be long upon the land." [2] Much of the Old Testament records not so much that which was done wrong, but rather that which was the horrible consequence of not doing right. Yet, at the same time, much of it also, even when looked at on its own terms and not with an eye to what we, with our vested interests of centuries later, would like to find, is moral in a very pure sense. There are good reasons for this. For one, the great deeds that their God could do for the Hebrews, He had long since done in leading them out of Egypt into the land of Canaan. Any further favors which they, by appropriate entreaties and sacrifices, could induce Him to bestow could not lessen the debt of gratitude and service which they already owed to Him. From that far-off time they were bound to keep

their half of the Covenant and to obey His commandments.

Furthermore, and some may find this more persuasive,
when the Hebrews settled in the new land, a completely
homogeneous community did not result. Instead, there grew
up a contrast, ever more apparent, between the ethics and
the social organization of the new cities: the kings and
their palace guard and court circles on the one hand
and, on the other, the older, simpler, more rigorous ethic of
the nomadic life which, in the time of Moses and the Covenant, all Hebrews had shared and which, in later years,
some few persisted in conserving both as a proper way of
life for themselves and as a memory of things past and
sacred for the whole nation. Add to this contrast the external threat, and it becomes practically inevitable for "The
words of Amos, who was among the herdmen of Tekoa" to
be "Woe to them that are at ease in Zion, and trust in the
mountain of Samaria. . . . That lie upon beds of ivory,
and stretch themselves upon their couches, and eat the
lambs out of the flock. . . ." [3] The very stuff of the
Hebraic tradition provided all the ingredients necessary
to the voicing of protest, social protest against wrongs done
by the mighty to the poor, moral protest against the wickedness of wanton luxury and self-gratification, and, above
all, moral and social protest by individuals against the
prevailing order. The Hebraic tradition has always been
individualistic at least in the sense that from its earliest
memories it has provided the moral basis for the radical and the revolutionary.

But, however characteristic and necessary the tradition
of individual protest may have been to the whole history of
Hebrew religion and however important it may have continued to be in later ages, it remains true that, until the

Exile, what Amos, for example, castigated was "them," the children, the House of Israel. Without exception the iniquities singled out for condemnation—incorrigibleness, oppression, idolatry—are all those of the tribe which is assumed to be and to act as a unit. The criteria within which the judgments are passed are all tribal. The covenant they have broken is the one "they" made, and the God they have offended is considered, with the exception of only one or two very general hints to be the god only of "their" nation. It was Amos, a mere herdsman, who protested, who passed judgment on the socially powerful, and the audacity of his individual initiative should never be underestimated. But the religion and its central concern were still tribal, and all this hardly more than a century and a half before the fall of Jerusalem.

In Jeremiah, a prophet who not only foretold that catastrophe but who also had to live through it and deal with it when it came, we find the faint beginnings of a shift away from sole concern with the tribe and its actions to more personal problems. The whole of the attitude which Amos so well represented earlier is still present, but the shock of events has forced accretions which, in part at least, contradict it. The most obvious of these reflect changed assumptions about the nature of Yahweh. Jeremiah recounts that the Lord said to him, "Behold, as the clay is in the potter's hand, so are ye in mine hand, O house of Israel." This could be taken to express no more than the old and familiar relationship between the tribe and its particular divine provider and protector. But the implication in this statement that the Lord is absolute, master of Israel only as He is also master of all history, is drawn out and explained by the words which immediately follow it: "At what instant I shall speak concerning a nation, and concerning a kingdom, to pluck up, and to pull down, and to destroy it. . . ." [4] There are frequent examples of this kind of thinking in Jeremiah, and they represent the feeling which many Jews must have had at this time: the fate of their nation could not be explained in the old, narrow terms. Yahweh now could only be understood as acting on a stage whose dimensions were not limited by national geography.

The logical corollary of this attitude is that, since Yahweh is coming to be thought of as a universal god, one need not necessarily have recourse only to the temple and the sacrificial rites of the Jewish tribe to have relations with Him. The practical argument in this same direction was equally compelling: He had visited his wrath upon the nation, and it remained only for the scattered population to make such individual peace with Him as they could. Both arguments push the necessity of establishing a personal relationship to God, and Jeremiah is perhaps most usually noted for the evidence he supplies that in his time this necessity was beginning, however unself-consciously, to be appreciated. Some of this evidence is engagingly frank:

Righteous art thou, O Lord, when I plead with thee: yet let me talk with thee of thy judgments: Wherefore doth the way of the wicked prosper? wherefore are all they happy that deal very treacherously? [5]

This is not only personal in the directness of the inquiry. It is also personal in the more profound sense of showing a man who wishes to get things straight in his own mind. [6] This is an attitude which is typical of at least parts of the book of Jeremiah, and it is one which can only be described as prayerful. We know it was at this time that, generally, individual prayer came to be recognized as a usual form of religious worship for the Jews, a form significantly independent of any need for the traditional and tribal rituals and surroundings. Specifically, we know that Jeremiah not only prayed a great deal himself; he also, in his letter to them, commended prayer to the exiles.[7] Prayer, perhaps more than any other act a man can undertake, is individual and private. It is the means by which a man, in the privacy of his own being, seeks to know and to receive into his own mind the ways of his God. Certainly, the subject of the prayer may be the collective tribe and its collective fate. Much more often than not, this was the case with Jeremiah. The formulation of purely private concerns had not yet come about. But, the activity of praying is a private one, and its growing utilization at this time shows that the basic loyalty was shifting away from being "through nation to God" to a direct loyalty to God. The tribe was gradually becoming simply the environment within which each man, having sought out for himself the will of God, then performed it as individually directed.

Thus was begun the process in Hebraic history by which the individual was shaken loose from some of the too binding ties of tribe and nation. Yet what has been noted here so far are only beginnings. The major emphasis of the religion actually practiced in the years of Exile was distributed almost equally between the more public matters of elucidating the Law, seeking the restoration of the Temple, and proclaiming the Messianic hope. The developments on the one hand, of a conception of a truly universal God of all history and, on the other, of attitudes, expressed in the act of prayer, which increasingly saw the individual as alone and in direct communion with that God, are no more than seeds. They are understandable best in the context where they originated, but they did not grow into the substance of a personal religion until after a long period of slow development.

The parallel, though much later, process by which the Greek cities lost their independence is much better known in modern schools than is the story of the destruction of the kingdoms of Israel and Judah. The name of the conqueror of Jerusalem may be known fairly widely but, if it is, probably the reason is that Nebuchadnezzer is such a fine name and appears in the refrain of a popular spiritual. But such fame cannot compare to that of Alexander. Alexander is known, known to have wept when no lands remained for him to conquer, known to have died young. It is widely understood, too, that the empire which this world-ordering young man created marked the end of the city-state. The Periclean Ideal remained to trouble and to distract both conservatives and utopians. As an ethical and social ideal it is still with us. But philosophers then and ever since have known, in their minds if not in their hearts, that men would have to learn to live both by themselves and in a cosmopolitanism increasingly universal. In the wake of Alexander the Great, Stoics, Cynics, and Epicureans, though their ways were different, all sought to fashion philosophies which would take account of the new conditions of empire.

This Greek response to changed environment developed in the same general pattern which we saw beginning, some two and a half centuries earlier, in Hebraic history after the fall of Jerusalem. Just as Judah was not utterly destroyed, neither were the city-states of Greece. They were conquered, their walls often dismantled, but they were allowed to retain control over a considerable measure of their local affairs. In fact, the Alexandrian policy of Greek and Eastern mutual assimilation prompted the attempt to dot much of the new empire with cities established in frank imitation of the Peloponnesian model. But, and again this is similar to Jewish experience after the Exile, the changes in social organization caused by the loss of sovereignty worked great modifications in the realms of ideas and beliefs. The remaining old cities and the newly established imitations no longer provided practical examples of the self-sufficient cultural units presupposed by the Periclean Ideal. They were now all contained, and would continue to be contained until at least the fall of Rome, within the aegis of some one or another great and comprehensive and distant government which imposed upon whole groups of them the common identity of vassalage, however variously arranged. Such individual independencies and differences as the cities possessed were only tolerated because found administratively convenient. In the light of this situation, the task of the philosophers could no longer be to explain and extol the needs and ways of the isolated and self-dependent social organism. Rather their task had become to express and to justify a life purpose for the individual, now lonely and often wandering from city to city within empires so large that he could no longer even conceive of regarding all his neighbors, wherever he might meet them, as "fellow citizens" in old communal sense of ancient Athens.

In the responses the philosophers made to these demands, we can see the familiar tendencies to turn inward, away from the community, to a greater concern for the fate of the individual and, at the same time, to look outward, beyond the community, for a more permanently and universally sustaining justification of life. Some of the evidence for this we have already had occasion to note. Plato and Aristotle, by retiring to their "private gardens," [8] revealed that for them, personally, despite all their protestations in favor of the political life, concerns other than that of the statesman demanded their attention. The statesman acts: Plato and Aristotle, most of the time, contented themselves with contemplation. They still often contemplated the local city-state; yet, when this was their subject, they sought to understand it and justify it in terms far broader and more eternal than the traditions, customs, and religion of the city. Both Plato and Aristotle owed to the Sophists more than they cared to admit, not only in their relative unconcern with merely local criteria of right and wrong but also in their persistent interest in the universal character of man, nature, and truth.

The Epicureans, a school established shortly after the death of Aristotle, exemplify best the withdrawal from the city, its life, and standards of duty. From civic idealism they turned, via materialism, to hedonism, though, of course, it was hedonism of a very refined sort. But our interest in these people is not with the absence of idealism in their thinking nor certainly with the precise character of their hedonism. Rather it is with the fact that for them the only virtue, the only good, was the happiness of individuals and how they interpreted this. Aristotle, and no doubt most of the classical Greek philosophers, assumed that individual happiness was the final good, but, in the *Politics* at least, Aristotle insisted, in keeping with the Athenian tradition, that this happiness could be obtained only in the life of the good citizen. What set off the Epicureans and what is, indeed, surprising about them even for us to this day, was their insistence that the wise man could and should always attempt to find his happiness exclusively from within his own resources. The requirements of self-sufficiency and isolation, which the classics presupposed for the happy city, the Epicureans applied to the narrow compass of individual self-satisfaction. Though the two positions are easily and perhaps necessarily related, the Epicureans did not need to be materialists in order to be hedonists. When a man sets out, as the Epicureans recommended, to cast out of his mind all inherited belief, all customary religion, all traditional standards of ethics, to brand everything his community has taught him as sham, superstition, and probably malicious lie, and then turns to look only within himself for direction and purpose, all he can hope to find there are the promptings of impulse and appetite. Hedonism, or, more appropriately, "Epicureanism" as that word is popularly understood, was not the essential quality of the Epicurean philosophers. Their hedonism was merely the quality which identified them for what they really were, the absolute individualists of their age.

It is not hard to understand why they were such individualists, particularly if we bear in mind that their hedonism took the form more of avoiding pain than of pursuing ecstatic pleasure. They were the lost citizens of the early empire. It is as if, with the roof blown away and the walls torn down, they abandoned the hopeless task of repairing the house and sought only the comfort of whatever spark still burned on the hearth. They turned their backs on the grand uncertainties of the new order so that they might better seek the surer contentment of warming their bones. They symbolized, some have said, the post-Alexandrian "failure of nerve," but, even more, they revealed the distance that was opening in the Greek world between the individual and his community.

The Epicureans, of course, were not the only individualists of this age. The whole of the Sophistic movement, broadly interpreted, and all the questioning which it promoted of the usual and the accepted was individual-centered. It might well be argued that, in all this, the Cynics better deserve the title of pre-eminent individualist. Certainly they practiced a more thoroughgoing renunciation of community, for they, unlike the Epicureans and others, never organized their "withdrawal" into a "school" by which to ensure themselves a measure of institutionalized comfort and security. Rather, they were mendicants. Their condemnation of all the standards and distinctions offered by society was more violent, as their name has ever since implied. But it is the very violence of their protests that denies them the questionable honor of being simply individualistic. The Epicureans, so self-centered, so keen on the ideal of absolute self-sufficiency, were indifferent to the claims and needs of any society outside their own exclusive group—and there is nothing so corrosive as indifference. In contrast, the Cynics, negative as they may have been, needed society if only to condemn it. And more than this. They condemned, wholesale, the provincial, petty, narrow-minded society which they saw around them. They condemned even more the ignorant, gullible masses, mostly poor, who allowed themselves to be trapped by the restrictions and inequalities of the local community. In their condemnations, in their very negativism, there was always implicit the picture of a new society, universal, free, and in which all men would be absolutely equal. Like the Epicureans, they were individualistic, but, unlike the Epicureans, they set the individual not within the seclusion of some private school but in the domain of an envisaged society of all humanity. They determined to clear out the wreckage of the old and, in so doing and without really noticing, they prepared the way for the new. But, because of their congenital "cynicism," they could not put their vision of what was to come in anything other than occasional utopian terms.

The process, in both Greek and Hebraic history, of shaking the individual loose from his local community set in motion the twin tendencies by which he was at the same time individualized and universalized. But much remained to be done. The individual had begun to *act* individually:

in the Hebraic tradition, to pray directly to his god; in the Greek, to seek self-satisfaction from within his own personal resources. But in neither case can the individual be said to have become deliberately conscious of himself as an independent, autonomous being.

Nor was there yet a genuine public willingness, in orthodox philosophy, religion, or law, to accept the individual as individual in both fact and idea. The reactionary forces were still strong. In Israel, the call for the restoration of the old, the nation in the homeland, was insistent and durable. The Greek parochialists could number among their allies the greatest philosophers. And the first individualists were not and did not feel themselves to be in any way integral parts of the forces, Babylonian or Alexandrian, which had given them their opportunities. With considerable justification, they regarded themselves as victims of the forces of the empire and turned to individualism only in bitterness and retreat. There was no alliance yet between the new outlook and the new social and political order which had made that outlook a practical necessity.

At this early stage, therefore, there was no positive recognition of the individual on either the personal or the public level. When this recognition came, its most important forms, for the later history of the West, came on the first level from the Hebraic development of a truly personal religion and on the second from the ultimate development of the institutions around Roman citizenship.

B

The Hebraic contribution to this process of recognition drew strength from powerful and ancient roots. It took the form of providing a substance and vitality around which could be erected later the more rationalistic conceptions stemming from the Greek philosophers. The Hebraic notion, discussed earlier in another connection,[9] of the vital individual, an undifferentiated, total "soul," alive and acting necessarily within the dimensions of a historical context, an energy which, from its very nature, must seek to relate itself and be related to some cause or god or other object of loyalty, contributed a basis upon which much could be built. The contrast between this notion and that of, for example, the Epicureans, is again relevant. For these Greeks, the individual can only be visualized as an empty shell which, by the judicious and simultaneous maximization of marginal pleasures on all fronts, might achieve a state of self-suspending stability while the outside world crumbled and caromed round about. None of this for the Hebraic *nephesh*. That soul must live, and it must live in and with the world.

Jeremiah, during the Exile, signaled the first separation of this unit of energy, the individual soul, from the larger *nephesh* of the tribe into which it had traditionally always coalesced—and would again as easily unless it could be otherwise occupied. But the tendencies drawing the individual back, the hopes for the re-establishment of the tribal community as a sovereign, victorious nation, though never extinguished, were dealt by events a series of staggering blows which had the effect of freeing many Jews to seek that other occupation. The Exile was long and the return brought pitifully incomplete realization of all the dreams. Conquered and reconquered, a brief period of no more than puppet independence, futile rebellion—all these were thrust against the hopes of national redemption. The advent of Rome was probably the most deadening experience of all. A great, distant, and apparently limitless power, it must have seemed to level permanently the walls of petty nationalism and open up instead a vast concourse along which went all men, all impersonally subject to distant Rome. By the time of Jesus, the Jewish nation, even as a religious community in service to the traditional god, had broken into fragments of competing sects.

At the beginning of this period of steady disillusionment for traditional hopes, we find the first genuine hints of a recognition of a private occupation for individuals, one unconnected with the tribal occupation of national redemption. They appear in the work of Ezekiel, a prophet who lived among the exiles: the passage begins

The word of the Lord came unto me again, saying, What mean ye, that ye use this proverb concerning the land of Israel, saying, The fathers have eaten sour grapes and the children's teeth are set on edge? As I live, saith the Lord God, ye shall not have occasion any more to use this proverb in Israel. Behold, all souls are mine; . . .

and goes on:

Yet say ye, Why? doth not the son bear the iniquity of the father? . . . The soul that sinneth, it shall die. The son shall not bear the iniquity of the father, neither shall the father bear the iniquity of the son: the righteousness of the righteous shall be upon him, and wickedness of the wicked shall be upon him.[10]

Elsewhere in his book, Ezekiel, in his denunciation of the children of Israel—some of which must be as graphic as anything anywhere in the Bible—in his long recitation of the vision of the restored Temple and of the return of the tribes to their former domains, shows himself to be as imbued as any with the poignant communal hopes of the enslaved people. But in the passages quoted a very different note is struck. It must have been comforting, no doubt, to the captive Jews to be told that they would not "any more" be punished for the sins of their fathers. At the same time, these words of Ezekiel imply something much more important. The Lord says "Behold, all souls are mine" and the only standards he will use in judging them, each of them, are "the righteousness of the righteous" and "the wickedness of the wicked." *Personal* redemption, in this passage at least, is the sole concern. Jeremiah had taught the possibility of establishing a direct personal relationship with God. Ezekiel taught that there was good reason for doing so. He laid upon each individual the burden of personal responsibility. He put to each man the notion that each is the author of his own acts and is therefore confronted with the task of individually squaring his own accounts with his God. It may have been comforting to know that the individual would not share in the consequences of the nation's misconduct, but it must also have been disquieting to learn that the only way to the Lord's beneficence was through individual effort.

This personal concern appears only peripherally in Ezekiel. By the end of the period of Hebraic history that we are here considering, by the time of Jesus, when disillusionment in the old hopes was profound, this concern not only had become central but also was being taught, by powerful instruction, as constituting *the* primary concern proper for all men.

There are two broad ways in which the individualistic, the intensely personal element in the Gospels can be demonstrated. Both cover familiar and much-revered ground, but both require the continued application of the "merely" historical and narrowly selective technique which we have been using all along in these matters. In the present instance, this method must involve a dispassionate attempt to discover the meaning of Jesus' life to Jews of his own era. For this purpose, it is inevitable that the emphasis should be much less on the notion that Jesus was the founder of a great new religion, and much more on the idea that his teachings were a logical step toward the ultimate development of a universalistic individualism, which had commenced with Jeremiah at least six hundred years before and which cannot be said to have reached full maturity until four hundred years later.

The first way to reveal this aspect of Jesus' teachings is to note the historical character of his Christhood. Specifically, this means relating not the life of Jesus but the story of it as told in the Gospels to that propensity in the Hebraic mind to seek out an object of loyalty, to ask "*Who* is god?" From this point of view, proclaiming the "good news" that Jesus is the Christ becomes quite literally the first intent of the New Testament. The image of the Christ, the coming savior of Jerusalem, was, by the time of Jesus' birth, already some nine centuries old, while the related figure of the tribal leader who, through his communion with Yahweh, accomplished great things for the nation antedated even the legendary Moses. The Christ which tradition foresaw was a remarkable man, of the line of David, whose attributes of divine leadership would, after much suffering for past transgressions, overwhelm the enemies of Israel and make her first of all nations with peace, prosperity, and spiritual cleanliness for all:

Therefore the Lord himself shall give you a sign; Behold, a virgin shall conceive, and bear a son, and shall call his name Immanuel. . . . The people that walked in darkness have seen a great light: they that dwell in the land of the shadow of death, upon them hath the light shined. . . . For unto us a child is born, unto us a son is given: and the government shall be upon his shoulder: and his name shall be called Wonderful, Counseller, The mighty God, The everlasting Father, The Prince of Peace. Of the increase of his government and peace there shall be no end, upon the throne of David, and upon his kingdom, to order it, and to establish it with judgment and with justice from henceforth even for ever. . . . And he shall set up an ensign for the nations, and shall assemble the outcasts of Israel, and gather together the dispersed of Judah from the four corners of the earth. . . . the house of Israel shall possess them in the land of the Lord for servants and handmaids: and they shall take them captives, whose captives they were; and they shall rule over their oppressors.[11]

These words of Isaiah date from the eighth century before Christ and the writers of the Gospel were anxious to stress that their Christ, Jesus, conformed to the pattern so long foretold: the remarkable manner of his birth; the repeated and detailed exposition of his capacity to accomplish, in the miracles, what no ordinary man could; and, most revealing of all, the Transfiguration in which Jesus is seen conversing with Elias and Moses. All these are "signs" of the traditional sort. But there was, of course, the one great difference. When the question is finally put and the answer, "Thou art the Christ," "The Christ of God," [12] is given and confirmed, there is each time the foretelling that he will be killed. Jesus shocked the Jews in many ways, particularly and significantly in his attitude to the Law, but his claim that the Christ would die could not but have been the most shocking of all. Even Peter sought to remonstrate with Jesus on this point and received for his temerity the famous "Get thee behind me, Satan: for thou savourest not the things that be of God, but the things that be of men." [13] There is much that is positive in this and even more in the Resurrection, the victory over death, also foretold, but it is the negative meaning in it which is important at the moment. The Christ of Jesus who died could stand only as a repudiation of all the hopes of national redemption and, too, of all the dreams of individual prosperity which such a national redemption would bring. In repudiating these, Jesus repudiated just as emphatically the very notion of the nation, of the nation as constituting a single soul and of the nation as being a proper object of concern. All this is Hebraic, and the full measure of the crisis which Jesus brought to the Jews can only be appreciated in terms of the Hebraic tradition. But the fact that this is true and yet that Jesus could repudiate one major part of that tradition, shows how far, for him and his followers, the center of interest in the story, that drama which the Hebraic mind saw in life on every hand, had shifted away from the *nephesh* of the nation.

That their center of interest had become the individual, a source of activity and fascination upon which the Hebraic mind could, if it chose, fasten as easily as it did upon the nation, is revealed by the other method of demonstrating the personal element in the Gospels. Here all that is required is to look with no more than a minimum of objectivity at the actual teachings of Jesus as they are given in the Gospels. The contrast between these and, for example, the wondrously detailed strictures of Deuteronomy is great. Jesus himself is said to have felt it: "Think not that I am come to destroy the law, or the prophets: I am not come to destroy, but to fulfil." [14] But the difference does not lie simply, though this is great enough, in that "the law was given by Moses, but grace and truth came by Jesus Christ." [15] The Sermon on the Mount, when compared with the sections on the laws of Deuteronomy and Exodus, appears new and different also because the object of the teachings is different. The older books assume the existence of individuals related within the group and are concerned to regulate what may be called, for comparative purposes, their external behavior. They are enjoined to do unto, or *not* to do unto, to be punished for doing, to build and orna-

ment the communal temple, to establish and show rever-
ence to the station of the priests, and so on. In contrast,
Jesus, in the Sermon on the Mount, is concerned hardly at
all with *doing* and almost entirely with the *spirit* with
which and in which the doing already prescribed should
be undertaken. His concern is with dispositions, with the
internal aspects of action.

Blessed are the poor in spirit . . . . Blessed are they that
mourn . . . . Blessed are they which do hunger and thirst after
righteousness . . . . Blessed are the pure in heart . . . . Ye
have heard that it was said by them of old time, Thou shalt not
commit adultery: But I say unto you, That whosoever looketh
on a woman to lust after her hath committed adultery with her
already in his heart. . . . And when thou prayest, thou shalt not
be as the hypocrites are: for they love to pray standing in the
synagogues and in the corners of the streets, that they may be
seen of men. Verily I say unto you, They have their reward. But
thou, when thou prayest, enter into thy closet, and when thou
hast shut thy door, pray to thy Father which is in secret; and
thy Father which seeth in secret shall reward thee openly.[16]

   We do not need to hunt and peck for evidence of this
concern for the inner man. Superficially, the Sermon on
the Mount may appear to be no more than a random collection of pungent sayings, particularly to those who read
it with the hope of finding the "fundamental principles"—
in the Greek manner—of the Christian philosophy. Nothing
of that sort can in fact be found in it. But it is easy enough
to discern in the Sermon patterns developed after the manner characteristic of the Hebraic temperament. Look for
action, for drama, in the Sermon and much can be found.
To take only the first part, it begins with the words just
quoted, which identify and welcome those who would follow Jesus, and goes on to lay upon them a mission: "Let

your light so shine before men, that they may see your good works, and glorify your Father which is in heaven." [17] Then follows a description—certainly not an "exposition"— of that mission, of "your good works." But this description does more than describe. If the way it proceeds is noted at all, it can only be interpreted as also intended to produce in the lives of those who listen a certain dramatic response. For this description begins mildly by enjoining obedience to the Law and then quickly adds, even "the least commandment" of it. In fact, the example of the self-righteous Pharisees must be exceeded. But, the description goes on, besides obeying the Law, obedience must be in a certain spirit and the examples given of this are progressively more difficult. And still beyond this, the follower of Jesus must rise far above even the Law itself: the Law says an eye for an eye, but you must turn the other cheek; the Law says love your neighbor, but you must love and bless and do good for and pray for your enemies as well. Finally comes the crushing blow, "Be ye therefore perfect, even as your Father which is in heaven is perfect." [18] Any listener who earnestly "lives" through this series of mounting demands, who conscientiously experiences the soul-therapy they provide and who can yet feel self-satisfied must be smug indeed. By all means let us be meek and merciful; by all means let us hunger and thirst after righteousness; but the question is, can we do it? This is rigorous doctrine and the question is earnestly put. But it will be earnestly received only by those who are already earnestly concerned not only with overtly *doing* but also with inwardly *being* good. This is not "being" in the Greek sense of "having existence" but in the Hebraic sense of trying to maintain, by heroic effort, a certain disciplined posture of the inner man. The impact of the Sermon on the Mount cannot be felt except by those who already are concerned with this particular form of the problem of self-discipline, and the more ferocious and tenacious the demands for this kind of inner self-discipline, the more personal, the more private, the more purely individualistic becomes the concern.

The writers of the Gospels were well aware that the Christ of whom they wrote was nothing less than revolutionary in postulating this strenuous and intensely personal problem for individuals. They were aware of the persistence of the doctrine that the individual found his identity, strength, and salvation only within the tribe. One evidence of their awareness is the rebuke to Peter over the nature of the Christ. More clear-cut evidence is given in the incident, related in three of the four Gospels,[19] in which the Pharisees, attempting to trap Jesus into admitting that his individualism implies total unconcern for the governmental powers of society, ask if tribute should be given to Caesar, and get in reply "Render therefore unto Caesar the things which be Caesar's, and unto God the things which be God's." No doubt this rejoinder has in the minds of the generations which have come after raised more questions than it answered, dreadful questions not only about what exactly did belong to Caesar but also about who had the authority to make the decisions in such matters. But one thing this statement obviously did insist upon positively: there is *a* part of man which does *not* belong to Caesar, nor to neighbor nor to anything which they either separately or collectively represent. That part, whatever its extent, belongs in the sole stewardship of the self wholly to God. Nothing could more emphatically reaffirm Ezekiel's embryonic doctrine of the absolutely personal responsibility of the self, for the self, to God. Nothing could more clearly draw a line beyond which the self could not be surrendered to the claims of society nor beyond which society's interference with the self could extend. That line, once drawn, could not be, in the West, undrawn. It could only be sometimes ignored.

In this summary of the development within the Hebraic tradition of certain aspects of individualism I have stressed the dynamic and intensely personal character of the contribution thus made. But I have also emphasized that this development was throughout essentially Hebraic in character. Even the "revolution" initiated by Jesus bears all the familiar marks: the emphasis on vitality, on the need to exercise the quality within man which we now call "will power"; the emphasis on the need to establish relationships, to discover a "true" God and do its will; the teaching of ethical lessons in the only manner of which the Hebraic mind was genuinely capable, by telling a "story" or creating an experience within which is revealed, not "stated," a right *way*, not a "truth." Jesus' revolution was indeed all that the word implies, but it is not too great an exaggeration to sum it up by saying that he insisted upon resolutely applying to the individual all the standards by which, in former times, the tribe had been adjudged to be stiffnecked, obstinate, intransigent, self-righteous, self-seeking, idolatrous. In effect, however tremendous the consequences both for the course of Western history and for the intellectual character of the religious traditions of which he was a part, Jesus did not do more than transfer to the individual alone the mission of loyalty to Yahweh, of keeping the Covenant. What had been national destiny became a private and therefore all the more demanding occupation. Certainly Jesus founded a religion which was markedly different from all the other, especially the Greek, religions of his era. In demanding absolute responsibility of the self to God he revealed man's innate unworthiness for the task and, therefore, the imperative need for God's love and grace. But even this has obviously Hebraic origins: Yahweh may have been, in the Old Testament, pre-eminently a god of wrath but he had always been a party to the Covenant, had always been concerned for those on the other side of it, and they, for their part, had always proved unworthy of his interest in them.

The importance of bringing out the Hebraic character of the Gospels is that to do so makes it much easier to assess the contribution they made to the ultimate evolution in the ancient world of a philosophy of individualism. Measured against what was to come, Hebraic individualism was as incomplete as Epicurean. What it lacked was the element of universalism, a systematic and rationally comprehended cosmopolitanism. The purely, even though greatly modified, Hebraic outlook was still too provincial for that.

There were, of course, aspects of the outlook represented by the Gospels which had long been developing and which would easily lend themselves to further development in the universalistic direction. Monotheism was by this time unquestioned among the Jews. There was one God and none other but false gods. But even here old habits persisted. The intensity of the personal relationship between man and God demanded by Jesus no doubt occasioned the easy employment of the phrases "*My* God" and "*Thy* Father which is in heaven." But it can at least be suspected that both the intensity of the relationship and the use of the phrases drew support from the long-conditioned propensity among the Jews to think of God as always "ours," never simply as God. When read simply on their own terms and without reference to the interpretations supplied by later minds, the Gospels appear to contain a strong strain of egocentricity. God was the god of each man. He was certainly no longer the tribal god. But he was not yet Everyman's God. Everyman was a too general and a too intellectual concept to exist in Hebraic thought.

The distinction may be fine and the point worthy only for debate, but when the same considerations are applied to the social outlook of the Gospels they grow greatly in significance. From the modern point of view, the enunciation given in the Gospels of the doctrine of rendering separately unto God and Caesar is quite extraordinarily simple. There is no awareness of the trying problems which would be created when that doctrine was put in serious conjunction with the two great commandments to love God "with all thy heart, and with all thy soul, and with all thy mind" *and* to love "thy neighbor as thyself." But the position of Jesus and his fellow Jews was in this respect a simple one. They could readily refer to God as "my God" but no one could expect them to refer to Caesar as "my Caesar." Caesar was simply Caesar, a distant source of great and remarkably lenient power providing a peace and order which the Jews could profit by and live within but in which they can hardly be said to have participated. It was not their peace and order, and beyond paying the tribute, the rent, it barely touched them. As a result, Jesus did not see his individualism within a context of organized society. He did not visualize the time soon coming when men could, in one breath, talk of "my God" and "my rights" and "my country." Jesus had escaped from the cloying confinement of the tribe but he was not yet *in* the Empire. The process of looking inward away from the local community had been carried very nearly to an extreme, but the other and twin process of looking outward beyond neighborhood to a universal system of order had only begun. As a result, the individualism of the Gospels was no more than embryonic. It was, in fact, not an individualism at all but rather a form of personalism, however dynamic.

Again the point should be made that this conclusion about the limited character of the social outlook of the

Gospels is tenable only so far as the primacy of the Hebraic character of the Gospels can be consistently sustained. If the universalism of later Greek thought had any kind of significant influence on the Gospel writers, then their "personalism" would necessarily have been transformed into something much more cosmopolitan. And a strong circumstantial case can be made out to show that the Greek influence was pervasive. By the time the Gospels were written, Alexander's deliberate policy of bringing together Hellenic and Oriental civilizations was already four centuries old. This policy, although Alexander's empire largely broke up after his death, was consciously continued by many of the various rulers of the Middle East. With the advent of Rome, it again became universal imperial policy, even if applied with relative leniency. The obvious results of all this effort to blend East and West were to be seen everywhere. Not only were cities of the Greek type established deep into Asian areas, but these cities frequently incorporated many of the most familiar features of Greek civic architecture: theaters, baths, and sports arenas. The Greek language was widely spoken. Indeed, not only were the Gospels written in Greek, but it is also probable that Jesus, while speaking the Aramaic of his native people, was himself relatively fluent in Greek. Finally, by the close of the first century A.D., philosophy after the manner of the greatest of the Greek philosophers was everywhere known and increasingly influential throughout the Eastern Mediterranean. The writings of Paul, composed even before the Gospels were, are, if not the most obvious, then certainly the most significant, evidence of that influence. Paul was more Jewish than Greek, more prophetic than philosophic. But had he not been as strongly philosophic and Greek as he was, the history of early Christianity would have been vastly different.

Yet these arguments are not conclusive. However prevalent, geographically, Greek culture may have been, there is very little evidence of its effects actually in the Gospels, especially in the first three or Synoptic Gospels. The Jews were particularistic, and their separatism, if anything, was intensified by their frustration and bitterness. No doubt, too, especially for them, religion would be the last area of life to be exposed to alien influence. The problems posed by the Gospels, we can insist, are purely Hebraic in form. Further, Jesus is portrayed by the Gospels as a man whose views were so broad-minded that he paid scant heed to the particularistic criteria by which Jewish tradition and society distinguished between men. Yet, he is not portrayed as being positively concerned to extend his mission beyond his own people. When the question arose some time after his death about whether Gentiles could become Christians without first becoming Jews, the matter was only settled after much stormy debate in the highest councils of the infant church.[20] The dynamic problem with which the Jesus of the Gospels confronted his listeners was a personal one for anybody, regardless of race or status, who cared to hear what he said. But the development of this problem into a general interpretation of the problems of Man was both a later and a slower process than is sometimes recognized.

A very considerable justification can therefore be advanced for describing the contribution of the Gospels to Western social philosophy in the limited language of personalism. In so far as the Gospel writers were non-Greek, were only Hebraic, they lacked the conceptual equipment to generalize their concern for the souls of men regarded individually. But, and this is the main point of all the foregoing discussion, it was exactly in this limited, egocentric, and essentially Hebraic form that the Gospels made their contribution to the full-fledged individualism of later years.

That contribution was of critical importance. The individualism which Augustine enunciated and passed on to the West would have been an arid thing had there not been at its heart a private occupation defined in terms taken directly from the Sermon on the Mount.

c

The framework of the individualism to come, within which the personalistic contribution of the Gospels could be deposited as substance, was provided by the development of the Roman Empire, both as a historical fact and as a practical concept. Many factors were at work erecting that framework, some of them causes, some of them means, some no more than incidental consequences of the Empire. Some of them, particularly in the realm of philosophy, displayed their obvious Greek origins. Others were as clearly indigenous to Empire experience. The mention of three of these various factors will have to serve to describe the character and extent of the framework for individualism which the Romans thus provided. These three, all of them contributing to that general process by which the individual as individual was publicly recognized, in fact and in idea, are the philosophy of Stoicism, Roman law, and Roman citizenship. The point to be especially looked for in these three is the way in which they, separately and together, marked out the structure of a philosophy which, while finding its ultimate purpose in the moral needs of individuals considered as such, was yet a philosophy of and about individuals *in* society.

This characteristic of being concerned primarily with the needs of the individual but yet always finding him in the context of a social order is implicit in the later developments of Roman law and Roman citizenship. In Stoicism, it is an obvious and deliberate feature. The Stoic school had been founded, as were those of the Epicureans and the Cynics, amid the wreckage of local loyalties left by Alexandrian empire building. But unlike these other schools, the Stoic school provided a philosophy which, while interested mainly in the individual and his new needs, yet deliberately saw him always within a context readily comparable with actual Empire conditions. The three major heads under which Stoic philosophy is usually discussed, Natural Law, the moral individual, and the universal community of all men, cannot be supposed to have been intended to describe the cosmopolitan and vast communities which Alexander and, later, the Romans actually created. But they bore so close a resemblance to what those communities, for one reason or another, aspired to be that it was easy for Stoicism to become for a time the favored philosophy among the men responsible for the administration of the Empire. Zeno, the founder of Stoicism, could not have intended that the master of all civilized men, Marcus Aurelius, nearly five centuries later, should have sought to live in accordance with the principles of Stoicism. But such was the historical "accident," and because of it and because Stoicism was therefore officially read into such enduring institutions as Roman law, a social philosophy of individualism, firmly established and widely accepted, stood ready to receive the dynamic impulse of the New Testament.

The avowed rationality of the first of the major aspects of Stoicism, Natural Law, is evidence of the debt which the Stoics owed the classical Greek philosophers. Both the Stoic and the classical philosophers claimed to perceive in nature an all-embracing rational order. But what Aristotle and Plato perceived was metaphysical, a constitution of being which rose to heights of absolutely rarefied pure form. This conception, in Stoic hands, is turned, in a sense, from the vertical to the horizontal and becomes thereby essentially ethical in content, a constitution for ordered life and history. The order is still cosmic, far beyond manipulation by man. It does not allow for variations in place or time. But in the Stoic conception there is an element of indeterminateness, allowing a wide opportunity for human obedience and error, which, at best, was only implicit in Plato and Aristotle. Rational idealism in the hands of the Stoics became the idealism of Natural Law in the sense the West still gives to that noble phrase. The Law of Nature is concerned not so much with the true and real order of the "is" as it is with the right order of the "ought." This has remained the case even though from the beginning the relationship between the two orders, without which Natural Law's imperatives would lose much of their claim to be "real," has been a source of bafflement and confusion.

Stoic contributions to the doctrine of Natural Law are not a development whose consequences can be deftly summarized in a paragraph. Even when regarded only as a contribution to political philosophy, the doctrine of Natural Law, by lending support to contract theories, to constitutionalism, to modern democracy in general, has been of an importance little less than monumental. Through Natural Law, the individual is armed against both state and community, and against the laws and traditions which these might seek to impose upon him, in a way and to a degree that in philosophy he never had been before. *The* Law, the eternal Law which no tyrant or mob, however fevered or powerful, could conceal or escape, the Law of Nature, there and forever, was rational. Any man, no matter what his rank or role in life, through the spark of reason in him, might see it. From this, an Epicurean, or other aspiring recluse, might draw comfort. Each man thus armed could plot and judge his own life apart from surrounding community. But Stoic theory could not faithfully allow such an emphasis. That theory was inescapably social and general. The rationality of both man and higher law which it insisted upon, made every man a judge, not only of himself and his own actions, but of society as well. For the Law is justice, and justice is the right order of society. The individual, freed by the doctrine of Natural Law from dependence upon all merely human institution for moral guidance, is yet, from the very character of that Law as law, bound to an interest in community.

The moral individual and the universal community of all men, the other major aspects of Stoic philosophy, are, in effect, commentaries upon the first principle of the relationship between Natural Law and man in society. The second of these, the doctrine of the universal community, was destined to be of more decisive and lasting importance. The claim that humanity constituted one community was an unavoidable consequence of the claim for the existence of a Natural Law whose essential reasonableness was perceptible by all rational men. By postulating one standard of rightness for all men it gave to them all an essential similarity both of purpose and of type. It was this which gave Stoicism its universality of scope. And it was this doctrine too, almost a mere intellectualism in doctrine but fully humanitarian in impulse, which acted as the bridge by which other, more dynamic, systems of belief crossed from narrow concern with personal problems to universal concern for the needs of the brotherhood of man. It was no accident that Paul, the Apostle unto the Gentiles, repeated the Stoic doctrine of the universal community almost exactly in the famous statement: "Now there are diversities of gifts, but the same spirit. . . . And there are diversities of operations, but it is the same God which worketh all in all. . . . For as the body is one and hath many members, and all the members of that one body, being many, are one body, so also is Christ." [21]

It is on the concept of the moral personality that Stoicism is weakest, historically and perhaps also theologically. In its theory, Stoicism suggested that all men, through their inherent rationality, could know the Law, could, therefore, accept the inner rationality of the world order, could discipline their appetites to this mold and remain undiverted by the apparent contradictions and temptations of this life. The necessary virtues were conscientious intelligence, fortitude, and devotion to such duty as was called for by individual station. But any doctrine, however universalistic in theoretical scope, however optimistic about the possibility of personal triumph, will obtain something less than universal acceptance as long as it relies so heavily on the rational faculties of man. The virtues of patience and forebearance, of calm, dutiful devotion to station were likewise exceptionable to the morally harassed condition of ordinary men. Though some slaves and others of the lower orders both understood and accepted it, Stoicism was chiefly suited to the established, prosperous, educated, and middle-aged who administered the affairs of the Empire and who could, through belief in and practice of Stoic principles, obtain for themselves a certain honor and self-redemption. This class was ubiquitous and its influence was powerful, both directly and culturally. Stoic principles became commonplace truths. But as a system, as a way of life, Stoicism could not but remain a doctrine primarily for natural aristocrats. It dignified the individual; it insisted upon the individuality of his moral personality; it earnestly sought to reveal and define the reality of his moral options. But the tasks which it laid upon him, however noble and refining, were largely appropriate to men not only already wiser but also more self-disciplined than the average.

But, as has been suggested, these beliefs, for one reason or another and in several ways, were embodied one by one in the institutions of Roman law and Roman citizenship. It is fortunate that they were. They otherwise might well have remained the airy possessions of the persons who actually subscribed to them as a whole faith. The institutions of law and citizenship took these Stoic doctrines and brought them to bear immediately upon the lives of men of all sorts and beliefs in all parts of the Empire. The ordinary citizen may not have known, nor could he be supposed to have much cared, where his beliefs in the rightness of the order of the world commonwealth, which Roman institutions more or less represented, came from. Often, he probably was quite unaware that he had them. But there can be little doubt that by the time of Augustus the notions of a Higher Law and of a universal community of moral individuals were accepted throughout the Empire almost without question.

This concretization and dissemination of Stoic doctrines was primarily the work of the imperial administrators. And it is important to admit that, however well versed they individually may have been in Stoic philosophy, their policies were also largely influenced by more practical considerations. They had to run an empire and in this they faced, *inter alia,* two great tasks: the first was to work out and get accepted a generalized conception and system of order which, in its discipline, would be everywhere the same; the second was to create a race of cosmopolitan empire-citizens who would respond to that discipline wherever and whoever they might individually be. Not even the Romans solved these problems to perfection. But they went a long way and along every bit of it they forced, against the continuous opposition of a parochialism to which they themselves on occasion contributed, a growing public recognition of the universalized individual. Sometimes the progress toward this end was deliberate, frequently it was unwitting, and always, no doubt, the motives were mixed. But the result, however intended, was the same: the work of the imperial administrators made a space in one corner of the mind of Western man for the conception and the image of the individual, alone and always himself.

The manner in which Roman law contributed to this concretization of Stoic, or at least Stoiclike, notions can be briefly summarized. That law began its long history as a "city" code, ritualistic, formalistic, based primarily on the *patria potestas* and applicable almost exclusively to the narrow class of properly born. This was the original *jus civile.* But Rome was destined to become something more than a refuge settlement on the summits of some easily defended hills. As Rome grew in commercial wealth and military power, her magistrates were compelled to develop a law with which to settle the disputes and to keep the peace among the increasingly numerous non-Roman classes—the resident aliens, conquered peoples, allies, and emancipated slaves. The law the magistrates developed for these purposes, the *jus gentium,* differed sharply from the *jus civile* which, technically, it was supposed to parallel. It relied far less on legal forms and looked more to the discoverable intentions of the parties. It was based primarily on the immediate needs of equity and the demands of "natural" justice. More important, it was applied to the individual as he presented himself without regard to questions of whence he came or of who or what his family might be. There was much in this which answered obviously to merely administrative convenience. A law which was to apply "fairly" and also equally to a large, mixed, often itinerant and as often primitive population could not rely heavily on the presence of official records, however kept. Nor could such a law question sharply the status of those who applied to it for justice. But philosophers, then and since, have been quick to note the assumptions upon which such a law must implicitly stand, assumptions about the equality of "persons" and about the universality of both "the law" and the community within which it is applied.

These characteristics of the *jus gentium* proved attractive even to the patrician-born. The old *jus civile* gradually absorbed them until ultimately the distinction between the two sorts of law became more and more formal. In the later centuries of the Empire, *jus civile* came to refer only to the local, positive law enacted as no more than secondary legislation dealing with the special requirements of particular areas. In effect, Roman law, standing only just below the divine *jus naturale,* became one law, ruling without significant distinction all members of the world (Roman) community. Stoic notions had become the assumptions on which the law of the Empire was based.

In less specific terms, the same kind of story can be told of the evolution of Roman citizenship. The shifts in the meaning of Roman citizenship were both subtle and deeply involved in the context of events in which they occurred. Moreover, the end product was an intricate overlaying of various meanings. But, however complicated it may have been in content, the final form of Roman citizenship combined all of the ideas and values which provided the structure of individualism for the West.

In the earliest stages of its history, citizenship in Rome brought very real privileges, political, legal, social, and perhaps economic. It imposed real burdens as well, especially in regard to payment of taxes and performance of military service. These burdens were all the heavier because the foreign element in the city, the Plebs, did not share them. The Plebs did not share them because, legally, Plebs were not held to be part of the city, in its political or its civil or its religious life. As they had no duties, so also they had no rights, neither of person nor of property.

This situation and its meaning for citizenship are both directly comparable to what prevailed in almost all the cities of the ancient world in which citizenship was allowed any significance. In almost all these cities, especially Athens, the citizen body jealously maintained its exclusive position. For them, the word "citizen" retained its connotations of participation in the clublike life of the closed community. But Roman citizenship was different, as different as Rome herself was from all other cities. The Roman citizen body, for a variety of reasons, was steadily expanded until it included all free men of the Empire. This process took nearly a thousand years and in the end the meaning of Roman citizenship had been radically altered. The meaning of citizenship within the city-state context which Rome herself had once provided was retained, but it had to take its place alongside the new meaning which imperial Rome gave to the word.

The first stage of this long evolution is that in which the Plebeian classes gradually forced the abolition of distinctions between themselves and the established citizens of the Patrician class. The Plebs gained equality of representation in the military and political institutions of the state and full legal protection for all their civil and commercial activities.[22] By the middle of the fourth century, the distinction between Patrician and Plebeian, except perhaps socially, was unimportant. The effective divisions were between rich and poor, rural and urban, between moderates and expansionists, between, on the one hand, the newly developing Patrician-Plebeian "nobility" presenting a common front for wealth and stability and, on the other hand, the poor masses led and largely controlled by Patrician extremists.

The general pattern revealed in the long series of events leading up to this development is a familiar one, especially, for example, to students of British Constitutional history. The "underprivileged" win not so much because they are more numerous or stronger—the issue is rarely solved by tests of arms—but because the strengths they have are indispensable to the fulfillment of the hopes which the "privileged" have for the nation or city. But the chief point for us to notice for the present study is that the rights sought, when at last won, though technically unchanged, come to mean something very different from what they amounted to when they were denied. The first advantage of citizenship in early Rome was its exclusiveness. Yet by its very nature, that was an advantage which could not be liberally shared. When the Plebeian classes obtained the status of citizenship, they obtained not something comparable to the clublike citizenship of Athens (though that is what they had sought) but rather something that was already well on its way to becoming much more directly comparable to citizenship in modern experience.

There were other factors in the Roman situation which were to underscore and further define this major shift in the meaning of citizenship accomplished by the Plebeian victory. The most important of these was simply the size of Rome. The Republic at the end of the third century was already ten times the size that Periclean Athens achieved. It had grown too big to be a club. Moreover, while the healthy club demands exclusiveness, it also must achieve a relatively high degree of equality between the persons within it. This equality the Roman Republic was increasingly unable to provide. The law knew distinctions between kinds of citizens, between *cives optimo jure,* who possessed all civil rights and all political ones as well, and *cives sine suffragio,* who possessed only the civil rights. More important, there were powerful oligarchical tendencies, both political and economic, in the Republic which worked to produce ever wider divisions of wealth and power. The constitutional arrangements in both the popular assemblies of those years were such as to throw decisively the long-term control of affairs into the hands of the wealthy and the few.[23] Even Polybius and Cicero admitted that the various executive offices of the state and the Senate, admission to which was restricted to retired magistrates, were controlled by the "nobility" for the simple reason that only the "noble" could financially afford to undertake the long *cursus honorum* which led to the highest elective offices.

The economic consequences of Rome's consistent success in empire building exacerbated the conditions which these constitutional factors created. The Republic, throughout its more halcyon days, depended heavily upon its prosperous and extensive middle class. It was from this social and economic stratum that the five middle classes of army centuries were recruited and their financial support assured. And, besides supplying in addition reliable and loyal administrators and other servants for service both at home and abroad, it was this class which gave Rome much of her internal harmony and stability. But Roman ambition squeezed the members of this middle class too hard. They served too much and they were unable to reap enough of the rewards of their city's successes. In fact, many of them were personally ruined by the advent of the Empire. The produce of their small rural holdings could not compete with that imported from the newly conquered lands or grown on the large estates which a few, profiting from the foreign wars, were increasingly able to amass and to work with slave labor. Many of those ruined retreated back into the city, where at least they could sell their often valuable Rustic votes for what the trade in the *Comitia Tributa* would bear.

The general consequence of all these strains was the creation, relatively early in the days of the Republic, of an oligarchy which, without any stated legal right, yet formed an exclusive caste, possessed of wealth, outward marks of distinction, and many hereditary privileges. There were rumblings and even crises, but the positive and regular direction of Rome's affairs gravitated more and more into the hands of an ever smaller circle.

The consequences for Roman citizenship were a good deal more complex. Obviously, the power of the oligarchy meant that, as a practical matter, citizenship, in the sense of significant, regular involvement in the political affairs of the community, became less and less important. Yet that is not the full story. Both Polybius and, later, Cicero were convinced that it was only because the Republic's constitution possessed in its two popular assemblies a "democratic element," to be combined with the royal and aristocratic aspects of its other parts, that that constitution was glorious and enduring. In terms of practical politics they have been proved wrong not only by subsequent historians but also by the events which followed close upon their own lives. But, honorifically, they were probably right. The law of the Republic proclaimed that every *civis Romanus optimo jure* had a vote, even though it conspired to make that vote, if it were a poor man's, mean little. Honor and memory of what honor once meant are, in these matters, often of more importance than fact. It was the honorific value of Roman citizenship which was to grow both vaguer and yet ever more significant in the centuries after the Republic.

The claim that Roman citizenship, in its political aspects, had this honorific value is dependent upon a distinction being made between the possession of a right and its subsequent exercise. The source of the distinction lies in the fact that the process by which possession of a right is obtained is an operation distinct, both intellectually and practically, from the process by which opportunities are created for its free use. The latter process requires very considerable powers of contrivance and is a never-ending one. The process of granting rights, however, requires only the fiat of "the authorities," whoever they might be, that the persons receiving the right are "worthy" of possessing it. It was this quality of recognition which the honorific value of Roman citizenship emphasized. Indeed, the effective denial of practical exercise in itself served to isolate and thereby enhance the fact of recognition of individuals as persons, as separate sources of decision, and, perhaps, wisdom. Athens granted citizenship, but in that city effective participation was usual. The individual, once recognized, was immediately drawn into the corporate life of the community and became, not so much a person, separate and privately directed, as a member, a part, publicly directing and being directed.

The quality of recognition of the individual in the political aspects of Roman citizenship during the days of the Republic was enhanced by the civil rights which remained significant possessions of the status. The civil rights remained significant so long as citizenship itself remained relatively restricted and comparable rights continued to be denied to noncitizens. These rights Rome, with its law, emphasized far more than did Athens or any of the other ancient cities.[24] They comprised largely the rights to legal marriage, adoption, testament, ownership, and the like. The law did not declare marriages, adoptions, and so forth, by noncitizens to be illegal. It merely, by not recognizing the agents involved in them, refused to guarantee, with the force of the state, their immunity from interference by neighbors or even by the state itself. Certainly the citizen, by having his marriage or ownership formally recognized, became legally burdened in ways he otherwise would not have been. Certainly also he thereby garnered advantages, some of them considerable. But all these duties and privileges of the citizen flowed as consequences from the recognition of him as a person who could marry, who could have children, who could own property, and then could be rightfully left to manage his own affairs. Because he was a citizen, he was recognized as being capable and was therefore to be granted some degree of immunity from interference. The citizen was a man who had business which the law recognized as being in some sense peculiarly his.

These tendencies in the citizenship of the Republic were carried forward by developments under the Empire. The citizen class underwent an enormous expansion and, because of this, a steady evaporation of all its remaining practical advantages. The Italians fought their way into citizenship while the status still meant something, but Roman military commanders were increasingly generous in conferring citizenship upon troops as reward for gallantry. Emperors found the giving of it a useful, even if little more than supplementary, device for inducing loyalty from important classes in the captured provinces. More and more, the expansion of Roman citizenship became part of the deliberate policy of unifying and Romanizing the Empire. Finally, in A.D. 212, the decree of Caracalla, *Constitutio Antoniniana,* at a stroke conferred the title on all free men of the Empire who did not already possess it.[25] The extension of the citizenship to all free men did not constitute a legal revolution. The once-cherished civil rights of citizens were by this time nearly all equally guaranteed in effect to noncitizens through the developments in the law. And the claim "Civis Romanus sum" such as Paul made in a criminal case gave in most instances only temporary and technical advantage. Politically, with the advent of Caesarism, citizenship meant nothing, and the economic advantages, which in earlier days had come the way of citizens resident in the overseas territories, had disappeared with the growth of a permanent imperial bureaucracy. But if the practical content of Roman citizenship had now been reduced to nil, the same cannot be said of its ideological significance.

On this side of the issue, the general policy, in which the decree *Constitutio Antoniniana* was simply a final step, was of immense significance. The Roman Empire was an extraordinarily heterogeneous collection of races, cultures, and political units. Racially and culturally this fact is obvious. It is less obvious that the political diversity of the Empire was enhanced by the policy, partly deliberate and partly occasioned by the absence of practical alternatives, which leniently allowed a large measure of local autonomy to the various parts of the Empire and particularly to the cities gradually added to the Empire over the centuries. In these areas and cities, Roman citizenship, when it was conferred on individuals or groups, for whatever reason, was nearly always a supplementary citizenship which did not deny nor even discourage activity emanating from local attachments or status. At the same time, Roman citizenship itself had long ceased to have any exclusive connection with either Latin race or even Latin ways, although Roman manners were much emulated in many parts of the Empire. The result was that Roman citizenship became a symbol of a higher loyalty for men of widely varying origins and beliefs, a badge showing immediate membership in the large community of the Empire despite secondary attachment to and status in local community. When all free men were made Roman citizens, they all became in effect dual citizens, citizens of the Empire and also citizens of particular places within the Empire.

The first consequence of this was that the unity of the *Pax Romana,* an objective toward which the imperial administrators had been working since the days of Caesar and Augustus, received a real measure of institutional recognition. But a second, if more rarefied, objective was also thereby achieved. The concept of the universal "City of the World," cherished by the philosophers, was given by the all-citizen Empire a concreteness it was never to enjoy again. The Empire comprised all men of the civilized world; those outside were not so much men as barbarians, and the exceptions within, the slaves, were regarded in much the same light. This embodiment, even if partial, of all men in one community was an enduring thing, far outlasting the power of the Empire itself. It was a staple of medieval thought and its epitaph was hardly written before the birth of modern times. It endured because men persisted in thinking in its terms, in terms of the community as being real, of themselves as members of it, and of there being a law, first the actual Roman law and then the Natural Law, to govern its members. Its primary significance was its impact on the developing philosophy of individualism.

When this conception of the universal "City of the World" received its first and at the same time most complete embodiment, the civilized world was ruled by an emperor whose rule was absolute and whose personal adoration was actively encouraged. The citizen of that world, therefore, was not, not even remotely, a "participating" citizen in the Athenian sense. Yet, as in the days of the Republic, the honorific shadow of early practice remained. And Roman law, again as in the Republic, did guarantee to all free men, and hence, after A.D. 212, to all citizens, those civil rights which worked so much for the distinctiveness, the separateness, and the honor of even the poor Roman citizen. But much more important was the impact of the notion of that dual citizenship which almost alone had made possible the actual institutionalization of something resembling the World City within the extraordinary diversification of the Roman Empire.

This notion of dual citizenship did two things for the developing philosophy of individualism. In the first place, it made allowance for the obvious and necessary attachment which men had to their neighborhoods, whatever their variety and "provincialism." But by putting alongside of that citizenship the higher, the Roman, citizenship it placed a limit on the extent to which local community could control and use its citizens for its own purposes and life. The local community not only had to cooperate, through its established institutions, with the greater Empire which contained it. It also had to admit, and make allowances for the exercise of, the loyalty which its own citizens had in respect to their Roman citizenship. A formal and recognizable division had been opened between neighborhood and the neighbors considered individually. They were all neighbors still but only up to a point. Beyond that point, they were each something else, namely, Romans.

And what, in this context, did it mean to be a Roman? In the answer to this question the problem assumes far greater importance than it would if this were merely a situation of concentric loyalties involving duties to both local and national communities. It is true that loyalty to Rome, even in some of the most refractory provinces such as Egypt, was widespread and deeply felt in a sense highly comparable to the national loyalty of the modern patriot. It is true also that what might be called the "official" philosophy of the Empire demanded a loyalty of this sort. As early as the last days of the Republic, laws were passed with the deliberate intent of reinfusing, particularly in the families of the nobility, the traditional morality and loyalties of the old Roman *Civitas*. Service, complete and selfless, to the greater glory of the great community was what was expected. But all these attempts to resuscitate the old virtues in the new conditions of empire were against the drift of the times and the deliberate substitution of emperor worship was a measure of official consciousness of that fact. The empire was too vast to be an immediate and idealized object of "national" loyalty. The business of running it was too much the private concern of the central power. The increasing use not only of professional administrators, but of barbarian mercenaries in the army as well, further enhanced the detachment of the ordinary citizen. More and more the empire lost its appeal as a historical object in the pursuit of whose destiny every man must cooperate. Instead, it became simply a condition, civilized and supposedly eternal, within which personal life could become the first concern of most citizens.

To be a Roman citizen in this context no longer meant to be a Roman, in the old sense of that word, however much traditional Roman ways were aped. To be a Roman citizen now meant, much more, to be simply a man, a *persona*, recognized by law, protected by law, an accepted member of the civilized world. The community of which he, as a Roman citizen, was a member was, indeed, still a community but it was one from which most of the communal, the neighborly qualities had been abstracted. It was a community of strangers. The bonds of it, of course, included the general consciousness that all free men, now that they were all citizens, were the heirs to the might and culture of Rome. But this consciousness, particularly as Roman power dwindled, served mainly to cast only an aura of importance and dignity around all those who called themselves Romans. Of more enduring and growing significance was the bond which came from the fact that it was in their Romanness that all these men, these citizens, found their essential equality. This was an equality which stood out despite all parochial differences, all differences of race, culture, and status. Their Roman citizenship was their claim, sometimes explicit, always at least implicit, to that respect properly due themselves as men, endowed with personal dignity and the possibility of personal purposes. In the eyes of the law, whether the actual law enforced by the state or the Natural Law supposed to govern from above, they were persons and were to be regarded as such both by their immediate neighbors and by the strangers they might meet on the long roads of the Empire. This recognition is what their citizenship brought them.

Not the least extraordinary thing about citizenship having come to have this meaning is that it should have come to have it at all. The new had developed from the old meaning of the word, but the two were in many ways antithetical. The old meaning, demanding participation as both the price and the privilege of exclusiveness, ensured the containment if not the complete absorption of the individual within the community. The new meaning not only opened a cleavage between the individual and his neighborhood. Having done that, it then insisted upon his individuality, the universality of his uniqueness as a person. Whoever he was, wherever he was, whatever claims might be made upon him, he was a person, not just a part, never just a "member."

However different the new meaning was from the old, it is easy enough to see that the new depended upon the old. Roman citizenship would not have come to mean something important unless it had "once" been important too, even though in a very different way. And it is probably true also that, except for the fact that the secondary citizenship continued to preserve the old meaning with something of its original practical vitality, the more general Roman citizenship, which permitted the secondary attachments, would have atrophied.

There is a further point to be noted about this new meaning of citizenship, one which binds it together with Stoicism and Roman law as parts of the general Roman contribution to the Western philosophy of individualism. The most important feature of this new meaning for citizenship was that it implied recognition of the individual and that that recognition was formal and public. It should be noted further that the recognition was not only genuinely *of* the individual but also that it was as genuinely recognition *by* society and its institutions. As such, this quality of recognition in Roman citizenship constituted the basis of a truly *social* philosophy of individualism. As spelled out and protected by Roman law and as understood and, no doubt, often practiced in the spirit of Stoic philosophy, Roman citizenship in its later forms can be seen as constituting the best expression of a whole outlook on man and his place in society. Viewed in this broad way, Roman citizenship becomes the symbol of the whole of the Roman contribution to Western individualism. This is the "structure" of "individuals *in* society."

On the other hand, it should also be pointed out that although Roman citizenship was truly a recognition of the individual by society, that recognition did not stem from, was certainly not occasioned by, any passionate recognition of the individual by himself. The Empire provided the structure, universal and to a degree institutionalized, of an individualism. But it provided no content. Almost backhandedly, it recognized the citizen as individual, as private, as alone in a large world. But it did not instruct him on what to do with, or in, his privacy. It hardly could. The "official" philosophy did not constitute anything approaching a positive, dynamic philosophy of private occupation. Instead, it preached a philosophy of public duty, even if toward the end, as by Marcus Aurelius, in weary and aridly intellectual terms. Of course for Aurelius the object sought was personal fulfillment or salvation. So was it also for Plato and Aristotle. And as it was for the Greeks, so also was it again for the noblest of Roman emperors, that the way to that goal was through the performance of the duties of public station. But there was little in that way to excite the ordinary citizen in the vast and impersonal conditions of the Empire. His way to salvation was perforce private. And the Empire increasingly "honored" this ordinary citizen by leaving him to discover such a private way himself. The definition, the practical scope, the need even of the private way, the private occupation, were all to be marked out by Christianity, a source alien to the ancient roots of Roman citizenship.

D

This brings us to the final phase of the development in the ancient world of a philosophy of individualism, a philosophy which was to provide the basic pattern of individualism in the West thereafter. In the first phase of that development, the individual was shaken loose from his local community when it lost its status as an independent, political unit. When the Hebraic and Greek communities were swept into empires, men were forced toward both a greater self-awareness and a greater breadth of view. In the second and third phases of individualism's development, there came a gradual but increasingly self-conscious recognition that the individual had been separated from his community, that he was, in some measure, alone with his private needs and personal fears. In the Hebraic tradition this recognition took the form of a personal religion which achieved its most dramatic expression in the New Testament. In the Greek tradition, individual recognition began with the post-Alexandrian schools, most notably Stoicism, and was carried forward into the Roman Empire and eventually embodied in the duality of Roman citizenship.

The final phase, which we now come to, took place within the great movement, largely Christian, which sought somehow to combine the divergent modes and purposes of thought of the Greeks and the Hebrews. A complete synthesis, as was suggested earlier, has never been achieved, and the intellectual history of the West, from Augustine, through Aquinas and Luther, and down to numerous modern philosophers, is in large part the story of ever new attempts to recombine what we loosely call rationalism and voluntarism.

But for the particular purposes of social individualism, the two traditions blended fairly easily, even if some of the permanence of that blend is admittedly due to the obstinate instability of the general synthesis. Here the problem was simply to bring together, on the one side, a doctrine of personal need, narrow in view but capable of the greatest intensity and, on the other side, a social outlook which was universal in scope but singularly lacking in internal energy.

Either, by itself, might well have died. The self-searching and self-condemnation demanded by the New Testament are tolerable for ordinary men only within limits. Likewise, the absolute idealism of doctrines of Natural Law and the Community of Humanity is simply too rarefied for common mortals to translate into practical terms unless these doctrines are attached both to mundane institutions and to personal needs and emotions. But together, the two views of man could both restrain and reinforce each other, and together they have weathered centuries of reinterpretation, reapplication, and re-emphasis.

It is sometimes remarked that the Romans, as philosophers, were not original, only eclectic. It is insisted that they merely modified and developed ideas and ideals gathered from the Greek cultures. This view has been rightfully criticized on the grounds that the modification and development—if such it be called—of Greek thought by the Romans was fundamental. Ideas, especially the important ones which are taken into traditions, follow events as explanations, justifications, and idealizations. The Romans did use primarily Greek ideas, but the events which they had to interpret were as different from Greek experience as Empire is from city-state. The result was a philosophy of the world the like of which had never been known in Greece. Much the same kind of observations can be made about the impact of Christianity upon the Empire. There was victory for the Christians when, after all the travail, their religion was adopted by the Empire. But there was also victory on the other side. Very nearly as much as Rome was Christianized, Christianity was Romanized. Rome gave to Christianity the philosophy of the World.

It is this other victory which should be noted first, because by it the social context, without which no individualism, however personally intense, can survive, was carried forward. The religion of the Gospels pointed to each man to say, "Here is your need and there is your God." In this it was miscrocosmic, but only potentially so. Roman culture could supply the intellectual equipment necessary to bring out this potential. As the early Christians worked their way into the broader reaches of the Empire, there grew up for the first time a systematic, Christian theology. The Lord God became not only My God of this, my present life. He came also to be regarded as the Supreme Being of a universe of being. This God not only ruled the world through the exercise of His will. He *ordered* it by His divine creation of it as a rationally ordered universe. And in this ordered world, *a* man became Everyman, a something which had not only life but also a soul, a distinct substance the nature and problems of which could, at least, be speculated about in general, even abstract, terms.

The intellectualization and universalization of Christianity did not, of course, happen suddenly. It did not receive its fullest expression until the work of Anselm and Aquinas. But it began, decisively and within decades after the death of Jesus, with the work of Paul. As an administrator, even if he lacked the true administrator's congenital fondness and pragmatic appreciation for rules, Paul did more than any to give the infant Christian Church its first sense of cohesion and internal discipline. As a missionary, he was determined not only to preach to the Gentiles but to accept them into the Church on the issue of faith alone and with as little reference as possible to the requirements of the Jewish Law. As a result, the Christian fellowship could not be thought of any more as just another Jewish sect. At this early date, Paul, almost singlehandedly, set the Christians firmly on the course toward building a universal church for all men regardless of race, nationality, rank, or previous creed. Finally, as a practical theologian confronting the problems of his faith as they arose in his pastoral work, Paul articulated a body of ideas which both conceptualized and justified his work as an administrator and missionary. And he put these ideas in highly durable language.

Paul believed, and he taught his fellow Christians to believe, that salvation is by faith alone. Faith is something much more than belief in or intellectual assent to the truth of certain propositions. It is an emotional response by man to God, the sloughing off of all selfish and worldly concerns and the reception in their place of God's freely given mercy and love. This doctrine was primarily opposed to the notion that redemption from sin and a life of righteousness can be obtained by strict obedience to the Law of Hebraic and Jewish tradition. To the Galatians, a group of Gentiles who had become Christians but who had later been misled by some proselyting Judaizers, Paul protested, "We who are Jews by nature, and not sinners of the Gentiles, Knowing that a man is not justified by the works of the law, but by the faith of Jesus Christ, even we have believed in Jesus Christ. . . ." [26] It was from this doctrine of justification by faith, by an act of placing one's trust or "love" in one object of devotion rather than in another, that Augustine later developed in great detail and preciseness the Christian form of Western man's private occupation.

Paul also taught the other side of Western individualism, the social and universalistic framework without which the doctrine of justification by faith would have shrunk into personalism. He regularly saw the various churches over which he claimed personal authority as living communities and he taught that the members of them should live in cooperative fellowship. To the Thessalonians, who were in some excitement in eager anticipation of the Second Coming, he wrote:

For even when we were with you, this we commanded you, that if any would not work, neither should he eat. For we hear that there are some which walk among you disorderly, working not at all, but are busybodies. . . . But ye, brethren, be not weary in well doing.[27]

From this and other passages it would seem that Paul had been influenced by the Greek conception of the organic community.

But of more memorable importance than this insistence that each citizen should pull his own weight in whatever community he happens to be is Paul's conception of the universal brotherhood. Perhaps he got this conception from the Stoics, for he had ample opportunity to learn from them both in his youth and after his conversion. Perhaps it stemmed from his pride in being a Roman citizen and from his appreciation, as a missionary, of Rome's peace, toleration, justice, and roads. Perhaps, also, and for many this is both the most obvious and the most reasonable explanation, Paul's conception of the universal church is simply the immediately necessary consequence to his doctrine of justification by faith. That doctrine necessarily as well as practically rejected all nationalistic or other parochial criteria for salvation.

For ye are all the children of God by faith in Christ Jesus. For as many of you as have been baptized into Christ have put on Christ. There is neither Jew nor Greek, there is neither bond nor free, there is neither male nor female: for ye are all one in Christ Jesus.[28]

And again:

Unto me, who am less than the least of all saints, is this grace given, that I should preach among the Gentiles the unsearchable riches of Christ; and to make all men see what is the fellowship of the mystery . . . . There is one body, and one Spirit, even as ye are called in one hope of your calling; One Lord, one faith, one baptism, one God and Father of all, who is above all, and through all, and in you all.[29]

These were the Pauline doctrines and their effects were soon felt. Christianity lost its purely Jewish associations and could make an unencumbered appeal to men of all sorts and conditions. More important, intellectual Christianity was able to take over almost without change, and then put to its own use, the intellectual conceptions supporting the whole scheme of Roman political organization, most notably the dual system of Roman citizenship. Every man was admitted, by Christian doctrine, to be living in some particular neighborhood, a community whose affairs demanded and should rightfully receive some share of his conscientious attention. But beyond these particular communities, every man was also a member of a greater community, the Brotherhood of Man. That community had its divine ruler, God, and it had a law, the law of God's Nature, rationally perceptible by all men. The duality of the Christian's status, a duality which was both to plague and to vitalize, was now firmly established. Emperors were especially suspicious and used the Christian profession of a loyalty higher than that owed the state as proof of subversive influence. But the emperors should not have been surprised. After Caracalla, the pattern of dual loyalty, of dual citizenship, was everywhere known. The Christians made a major substitution among the subjects included in the pattern but the pattern itself remained unchanged. For these were not Christians looking at Rome in terms of Christian ideas. Much more accurately, these were Romans accepting Christianity in Roman terms.

The absorption of Roman patterns by Christianity must not be underestimated. Christianity gained thereby not only in scope, but also that "eternal" quality of pure thought which, in Hebraic hands, it could never have acquired. Nor should the significance of these developments for individualism go unreiterated. The personal problem spelled out in the Gospels was dramatic and demanding. But if that problem was to have any enduring influence on modes of social organization it had at least to be included in some theory of society.

With the articulation of the philosophy of the Brotherhood of Man, complete with a sovereign God and a universal law governing all men equally, the personal religion of the New Testament acquired its social context. On the one hand, the second great commandment, to love neighbor as self, received a definition of consequences which, as a mere imperative about feelings, it did not have. After the pattern of Rome, this commandment now insisted that neighbor be granted that same respect for personal dignity and private purpose, that same immunity from interference, that the Christian citizen expected for himself. Love him, yes, and serve him but do not smother him for he, also, is a soul, a citizen. All men, and that "all" would one day be a cry from the barricades, all men are souls, are citizens equally in the community of God.

On the other hand, the conceptualized social context acquired in Rome by the Hebraic personalism put a bar before that absolute retreat into the self which, experientially, such a personalism by itself seemed to imply. The claims of public station were admitted and due allowance was to be made for their satisfaction. This was the import of the Christians' self-acknowledged double status. Not all were given to be like St. Francis. As a fact, that was true. But whether one argued for society from the premise of man's Fall or for the need of human authority from the perfection of order in all things, by Christian theology the workaday actual society was not only there but wanted. Some might be mendicants, but it would be unfortunate if we all conversed with the birds. There is a difference between being a good Samaritan when neighbor is found lying in a ditch and being a leading citizen, deliberately and consistently working with many neighbors. Both conditions do arise and are expressions of love of neighbor. But the first alone can be stressed in the Testaments. Emphasis on the second, an emphasis which might act as a more consistent bar to excessive concern with personalism, becomes possible only when the intellectual equipment is available to translate love of brother into the Brotherhood of Man. Only then can love for neighbor become respect for neighbor as equally a member of an actual community. Jesus said, "Render unto Caesar. . . ." Paul said, "Obey the powers that be. . . ." But Augustine was a bishop, an extraordinarily hard-working bishop who was never unwilling to take on governmental tasks sloughed off by a decaying civil administration.

This new emphasis which the Romanization of Christianity encouraged underlined the tension which was latent in the ethics which Jesus taught. The two great commandments were to love God absolutely and to love neighbor as self. The two are said to be "like unto" each other and, certainly, there is no outright contradiction between them. To love neighbor in the manner required is to love, or at least to demonstrate love for God. But two different relationships are demanded; one, as it were, vertical and the other horizontal. The various versions of Christianity have tended to distribute emphasis between the two "directions" in widely differing proportions. Some emphasize more the inward, the contemplative; others stress more the outward, the doing of good works. The intellectualization of Christianity that took place in the Roman era ensured that the second "direction" would never be wholly obscured. And in doing so, something of the immediacy of the first as it had been presented in the Gospels was lost.

But not much. However insistently it had been made clear that he was not alone, that he was ever one among many, the Christian still had his problem and he bore it with him into the Empire. Again, reference to Augustine is of the first importance. He was far more than merely representative and exemplary. He was himself, by his life and his writings, a prime force in shaping the intellectual history of the West. His often told quest for wisdom, which led him through most of the doctrines and faiths of his age, was perhaps only symptomatic of the cultural collapse of the Roman Empire. But the truth as he found it became in his hands absolutely firm. The pattern he gave to that truth, in his philosophy of being and history, was the intellectual pattern for the next thousand years. And at the heart of it all was the Christian definition of man's private occupation, the task, as it has been phrased colloquially, of "getting right with God." It was this which charged his philosophy with drama, with poetry. It was this, the role of the pilgrim, that gave to each man in the Brotherhood of Man a burden to carry, and one that, ultimately, each man had to carry all by himself.

The general characteristics of this burden were spelled out, by Augustine and many others, with an explicitness which sounds strange to modern ears. It presupposes an Hebraic understanding of man's nature. For other matters, man may usefully be regarded as primarily rational, or, as the case may be, social. And certainly in Augustine's rendering of man's final occupation, man appears as a far more "reasoning" animal than he did in native Hebraic thought. But reason, in Augustine, is no more than man's capacity to understand. It is clearly thought that behind that capacity to understand there is a force impelling man to seek the truth, to use his reason in pursuit of a vision of wisdom. That force arises from man's nature as a creature who loves, who must love, who must find and have and know an object of adoration. Man is incapable of being either neutral or merely passive. And the loving is thought of both as an activity, a doing, of the will and as an orientation of the soul. Love has both force and direction.

The first question given to man is, "What shall I love?" The Christian answer is immediate: Thou shalt love the Lord thy God, the creator of Heaven and of Earth and of man in His own image. Then comes the hard question: Can man love God? The Christian, the Augustinian answer to this question is a qualified one. Man has in him, innately, a love of God. Its first manifestations are man's natural love of knowledge, beauty, and innocence. But this love of man's is a weak thing. Love of knowledge, beauty, and innocence is a reaching out for the God who created them but it is no more than a reaching out. And, as such, it is always frustrated, turned back and away from God by another love also innately in man, the love of self. Pride can take many forms: obvious self-love as in desire for personal success, personal gratification, or, more devious self-love as in overweening love of country, party, family, or church. Its most important form appears when it is a perversion of man's first expressions of his innate love of God. Man can begin to love God but, as soon as that activity has demonstrated itself to any perceptible degree, then man becomes aware of his success, of the knowledge he has gained about truth and beauty. Worse, he is only too aware that it is he, man, who has gained all this. Instantly he is, in Augustine's own words, "puffed up" and believes that he can gain salvation, can learn to know and love God through his own unaided efforts. And this is the ultimate in pride. ". . . I pressed towards thee, and was thrust from thee, that I might taste of death: for thou resistest the proud." [30]

The Christian can come to know his self-love, to learn of its inevitability, of its constancy, and of his powerlessness to control it. He can, in part, come to an awareness of this through constant and strenuous introspection. But his final humility, his final conviction that he is unworthy, incapable of self-salvation, and therefore that God alone can redeem him, comes only with acceptance of the authority of the Christian tradition. For it is only within that tradition that, in the person and crucifixion of Jesus, God's redeeming love of man is revealed. To accept Jesus as the Christ, as the Lord of personal life, was to accept that He was the Son of God sent to die for the salvation of all men. At the same time, the acceptance of Jesus constituted a renunciation of love of self, a transference of that love to a love of God. Man could be saved. Man could love God. But this could only happen when both the futility of self-love and the reality of God's love were revealed to and accepted by man.

To argue, pro and con, the theology of this analysis of man's prime moral problem is simply not relevant here. It is enough to realize that this analysis was made and so authoritatively that it became an enduring part of the Western heritage.

But there are aspects of this analysis which are relevant and which need to be singled out for emphasis. One of these certainly is the very explicitness of the analysis. With that characteristic there is also its ready applicability to men of all stations and degrees of education and intelligence. As presented here, overly condensed, it appears dry and formal. But as preached and written by those who felt it immediately and deeply, by those who believed it the first problem of their own lives and not, as in the present connection, as merely illustrative and contributory to something else, the search for God's love and the defeat of self-love became an adventure of the grandest and most somber proportions. Any man who was in the least troubled with his own propensity for too great self-concern, who felt in the least the force of the imperative to live in terms of something outside of and more enduring and truer than mere self, would have a predisposition to accept the Augustinian statement of the problem as important, regardless of how he received the Augustinian solution. This was a private occupation which all men could accept as worthily their own. The questioning did not begin with abstract questions about whether God did exist or even could be conceived as existing, even though for centuries no one doubted the answers to such queries. The questioning began much closer to home, on a level far less arid. It began with "What am I and wherein lies my guilt?" Pride, it is sometimes said, is human nature. But equally universal is the acceptance that pride is a sin, that to love only the self, to put trust only in the self's views and needs, is the source of evil. Whether humble or not, we all, in the West, will agree that humility, whether before God or proper authority or simply "the evidence," is a virtue.

Besides the universality of the appeal of the Augustinian private occupation, there was another merit which his statement of it possessed. This lay in its energetic character. This quality stemmed in part from the strenuousness of the spiritual exercise which Augustine expected from himself and from all serious Christians. The search to find and hold God's love in the process of abandoning the pernicious love of self demanded constancy of effort and the full utilization of all a man's spiritual resources. Victory was always fleeting. For Augustine, ultimately, there was no such thing as a sure faith. Faith in God had to be ensured always by further effort to find it. But even this energetic quality of the personal problem of each citizen in the community of the Church stemmed from something deeper, namely, the basic assumptions which Augustine and the Christians made about the nature of man. For them, man could not be defined as simply reason, for that made him too contemplative, too passive to undertake the activity of sinning in the way and to the extent which they felt man did sin. Nor could he be defined as social, for that obscured the identity of each man's soul and its spiritual peril. Man was a creature who loved.

But to say that man is a creature who loves is not simply to say that man is pre-eminently will. Will, as we are so apt to understand it after the Kantian analysis, is "an uncaused cause." More exactly, will is that quality, condition, or power ascribed to a man when he is viewed as, or understood to be acting as, a moral agent. Taken coldly, this description has little force or directness, and gains hardly more even when it is added that we frequently do regard men as moral agents, and perhaps always should. The Christian view of man insisted upon getting far closer to its subject. It insisted, philosophical riddles aside, upon getting directly to the man, not as viewed, but as viewing. It dealt immediately with man acting, viewing, causing, loving. Christians would not have been deterred by any Kantian objection that such a man existed only within the unknown and unknowable realm of noumena. Life for them was not something to be viewed or understood. Life for them was to be lived. Man was, immediately, a source of energy. He was energy, a unique, individual unit of "*I*-am-doing."

This view of man was and is of enormous significance. Philosophically, no doubt, it is technically naïve. In origin, it is purely Hebraic and perhaps primitive, although it was to become a staple of Western philosophy. But there is no gainsaying its vitality. Give a Roman citizen, secure within the immunity of his lawful rights, this understanding of himself and a private occupation is inevitable. Give any man this understanding of himself, and have him hold it resolutely, and he will be undefeatable. To use absolutely, to submerge and contain within some system, any such "I," any such innately dynamic self, would require its utter elimination. This immediately energetic self is the root source of all modern Western notions of democratic equality. It is in fact the ultimate definition of the Democratic Man. Rights, freedoms, liberties, privileges—in a democracy all these are no more than instruments to let man *do;* not "be," but *do.*

There is a further aspect of the Augustinian definition of the private occupation which needs separate emphasis. This is its rigorously personal character. It is true that there is nothing in Augustine which in any way, even remotely, decries the character of the Church as a community. The Church is a community and Augustine's vigor as one of its bishops is sufficient evidence of his conviction that it is only as a strongly organized community that the Church can fulfill its mission. But at the same time he never lost sight of the fact that the Church's mission is with souls, is with men. Man's first activity, again, is loving, but loving is nothing if it does not come, directly and freely, from the soul.

In our age, liberals have proclaimed that you cannot make a man good. They have insisted that all the state and a man's neighbors can do is to provide the conditions within which moral action is possible. There is a moral obligation to provide these conditions, both physical and psychological. A minimum of personal welfare must be available before the moral life is even conceivable. But these limitations and obligations, profound and humane as they may be, which our liberals place upon the community and its state are meaningful only when the good which men must do is defined as emanating from an activity of the inner man, of the soul. A man can be trained and compelled to behave with social decency, to live righteously, and to cooperate with his neighbors. But he cannot be made to love. If it is held that man's first duty is to love well and rightfully, then it must also be admitted that this first duty is something which he can only do himself. The state can assist by providing the requisite material conditions and opportunities, the necessary instruction and exhortation. But, beyond that, it must leave the man to his own devices. On the other hand, disparage this Augustinian view of the essential activity of man, deny this understanding of man's inner person, and all the liberal limitations on the state will be as nought. If a man is only as good or as bad as his behavior, as he can be *made* to be, then the state will know no limitation. It will have every moral license to set about, with all the techniques which modern science provides, the business of making men good.

But the privacy of the occupation which Augustine defined for all men arose not only from the inherent individuality of the activity with which that occupation was primarily concerned. Everything that we have said about the privacy arising from that source would still be true, but how trivial it would all be if what Augustine had said was in effect that we should love our country, our native land, with all our hearts and with full loyalty and complete service. Augustine said that we should love and love is a private way. But he conjoined to that the imperative that we should love God, serve God, be loyal to God and then, after that, and in so far only as it suited God's purposes (as we understood them), that we should love and serve country. Community takes second place. Not only that. Community and state are not, for all their sovereign might, the final arbitrators of their own needs. The decision as to how far a man must serve his country is, by Christian doctrine, a decision to be made in the last analysis between a man and his God. The business to be dispatched between man and God is, from the point of view of community, private. Community can play, at best, no more than a subordinate role. It can provide the context within which man attempts to express his love of God (by loving neighbor) or it can provide the arena in which God seeks out the sinner. But it cannot do more. In sum, Augustine's private occupation, an occupation which the universality of his religion assigned to every man in the Kingdom of God, was private both because ultimately only the individual could pursue it and because its substance lay outside the province of the community's interests. Bishops and statesmen, working separately or together, could and should strive to provide the right environment. But the substance of what had to be done lay wholly within the relationship between every man and his God. Augustine sought anxiously the answers to many questions, questions about the nature of God, the nature of man, and the relationship between them. These were general questions, eminently suited to public discussion among churchmen and Augustine gladly debated them with any who would contend with him. But his anxiety to answer these questions was not a public thing. It was born, so he believed, solely out of the relationship between himself and God.

I sought anxiously "whence was evil?" What were the pangs of my teeming heart, what groans, O my God! yet even there were Thine ears open, and I knew it not: and when in silence I vehemently sought, those silent contritions of my soul were strong cries unto Thy mercy. Thou knewest what I suffered and no man. For, what was that which was thence through my tongue distilled into the ears of my most familiar friends? Did the whole tumult of my soul, for which neither time nor utterance sufficed, reach them? Yet went up the whole to Thy hearing, all which I roared out from the groanings of my heart; and my desire was before Thee . . . .[31]

The contention of this chapter has been that the tradition of the defiant citizen, who jealously secures his privacy by insisting upon his personal dignity and claiming all sorts of immunity from interference in his personal affairs, stems ultimately from a philosophy of individualism which took shape in the final centuries of the Roman Empire. The contention has been that this philosophy was centuries in the making and that it drew values and ideas from widely divergent sources. It consists essentially of two aspects. The first is an idealized social context within which the individual appears as an indissoluble unit and yet as also a member of the universal fraternity of men. The primary moral injunctions to be drawn from this aspect of ancient individualism concern largely the respect which citizens owe to each other as citizens and the extent and limitations of the service which the citizens perform for, and expect from, each other. Expression of these injuctions must rely heavily, in one way or another, on the notion of dual citizenship, on the notion that, while every man is properly a member of some present, actual community, yet he is also a member of another society, greater, more enduring, and more perfect than any in the immediate historical environment. This aspect of individualism is, in origin, Greek and, far more concretely, Roman.

The other aspect of ancient individualism is largely Hebraic and then Christian in origin. It insists primarily upon the existence for all men of an imperative private occupation. The occupation is common to all men, and the God they are to serve in it is one God for them all. But the nature of the occupation, the nature of the men who, it is held, must undertake it, and the nature of the relationships which are to be established within it are all such as to ensure its absolutely personal character. It is the kind of occupation which men can only undertake within the privacy of their souls. Furthermore, the moral value of this occupation is so great that its power to justify exceeds that of all other ventures which men can undertake.

It must be reiterated that, as the philosophy of individualism unfolded in the ancient world, its two aspects were always associated with each other. The general view which dual citizenship expresses is by itself not only weak but also incapable of providing much justification for the confusing status which it imposes. With a defined private occupation included within it, it achieved ethical respectability and firmness. By the same token, the private occupation as defined in Christian doctrines was saved from complete social unawareness and futility by more than those doctrines' own commandment to love neighbor. It was saved even more by the Roman environment, where that commandment came to mean consistent and constructive involvement in the daily ordering of regular communities.

There is a further point to be made about the material included in this chapter. What has been sketched here was an actual philosophy which existed in a particular cultural environment. As such, it displays a host of particularities and detail which made it very much a creature of its age. And only as such, only as thus complete, was it fully meaningful. But, for my special purposes, my interest in this philosophy has only indirectly been with its full meaning. In that full meaning I hoped to see a pattern. Cultural ideas change slowly. Many times they are changed simply by substituting a new idea for an old one within a whole cluster of otherwise enduring ideas. Viewed broadly, the intellectual history of the West reveals a consistency of pattern very nearly as great as the degree of innovation displayed with respect to content and application. It is only in terms of these observations that the philosophy of individualism, developed in the ancient world, is, for my present purposes, important. That philosophy provided a pattern of ideas which saw a social organization as legitimate only in so far as it took due notice of the private moral needs of individuals. It was this pattern, and only a little of the particularity of content, which was to ride down through history to the present day.

It is especially important to make this point in connection with the notion of private occupation. If the history of this idea were to be written, it would undoubtedly reveal that the theological connotations originally surrounding the notion have been largely retained right down to, if not actually including, our own day. But such a history would certainly also show that the theology included varied widely from time to time. And no doubt also the definitions of the occupation, the descriptions of the activity to be undertaken in its pursuit, would be shown to be so vastly different from what Augustine had in mind that he would have flatly repudiated them. One or two instances of this sort will be noticed in the next chapter. But however much variation of this kind might be found, the essential characteristics of the notion of private occupation have re-

mained remarkably unchanged. The notion of private occupation has retained its emphasis on the right of every
man to engage in private enterprise of some kind. It has
retained the insistence that such private enterprise is of
primary significance only to the author of it. It has retained the insistence that such enterprise is of the highest
moral value. And, not least, it has retained the insistence
that the private occupation is an enterprise, is an activity
of one sort or another, which men must be allowed to *do*.

Whether in the Augustinian paradigm or in later variations, the private occupation is not private because it is, or
can be, kept "secret." It is not private because it is personal in the same sense that some of a man's habits and
needs are said to be personal, others of them being in one
way or another less personal. Nor is the private occupation
private because the pursuit of it is, or can in some way be
thought to be, free of all consequences which might im-
pinge upon the interests of other people or public bodies.
On the contrary, no matter what actual task is set by the
private occupation, working at it will almost invariably
cause some public notice, will often require the resources
of the whole man and not just those of some personal side
of him, and it certainly may require at least the passive
cooperation and sacrifice of the community and probably
much more than that. What, in the Augustinian pattern,
makes the private occupation finally private comprises two
things only: it is some activity which does involve, or can
be understood to involve, the direct and self-directing
participation of the energetic "I"; and, second, it is an activity which is held to find its final justification and ultimate utility primarily in terms of its consequences for that
energetic "I." On these terms, the private occupation could
be exactly what it was for Augustine. It could also be, as
it was for many in the latter part of the nineteenth cen-

tury, the pursuit, through personal endeavor, of material wealth.

There is a final qualification to be added to all this. It has never been contended that the whole of this pattern of individualism possessed some exclusive and dominating position. By historical accident, during its inception in the last days of the Empire, it may be fairly said to have very nearly described actual conditions. But it would be foolish to assert that it again came near to determining actual modes of social organization until modern times. All that is contended here is that this pattern of individualism has remained constantly present, always more or less of an influence, always a pattern in which men to a greater or lesser degree arranged their ideas about man's place in society.

I V

INDIVIDUALISM IN THE

AMERICAN TRADITION

In so far as this book has a lesson, the substance of it consists largely in the mere presentation of three ideas—participation, service, and privacy—concerning what citizenship
should mean for the democratic communities of the West.
If the three ideas are taken together, citizenship implies a
duality which has been often noted but as frequently forgotten. The citizen, in our Western heritage, is held to be
both a public person and a private person, to be both in
and yet also out of society.

The material presented in the preceding chapters has
taken the analysis of citizenship beyond this usual point.
Most importantly, it has laid emphasis on the notion
that the citizen, whether in or out of society, is an actor, a
doer, that the citizen is a man who finds in his citizenship
an occupation, or rather, a triad of distinct occupations:
the citizen participates in the life, the activity, of his com-

munity; the citizen is loyal, serves his community, aids it in the fulfillment of its common mission; and, not least, the citizen, while admitting these other claims upon him, pursues his private destiny, works at his private occupation.

This emphasis has an importance of its own. By viewing the citizen as an actor and doer, citizenship is given a vividness and vitality which, in a democracy, it fully merits and which no number of lists of duties, rights, and privileges could ever provide. But of even greater importance is the fact that this emphasis enables us to go to some lengths to define and describe what it is that the citizen is supposed to do. As a result, the frequently noted duality in Western citizenship can be seen to arise not from some artificial division of the citizen into public and private selves. Rather, it is seen to arise from the fact that of the three occupations given to the citizen by the traditions of the West, two are of an essentially public character, can be performed only in public through a public life, whereas the third possesses an essentially private character, and ultimately can be performed only within the privacy of a man's soul.

A second advantage of concentrating attention on what it is that the citizen is supposed to *do* is connected with the reality that rights, like all practical institutions, are socially accepted ways of doing things. As such, they are always means. They are to be justified only in terms of the ends, the activities, which their possession allows citizens to undertake. Thus, if we know with some precision what we expect our citizens to do, then we can study, supply, rearrange, and then defend and justify the system of rights which we bestow upon them.

A third advantage of knowing as clearly as we can the nature of the citizen's occupations also deserves separate mention. The duality in Western democratic citizenship is not only well known. It is perennially troublesome. By knowing the complexities of the process by which citizenship developed, by learning of the divergent sources from which its various aspects derived, by realizing that Western citizenship is historically and irretrievably bound up with the perpetually unstable synthesis which is the core of our intellectual history, we can learn to accept the fact that this duality in our citizenship is incapable of quick or easy resolution. The troubles to which it gives rise are ones that we just will have to learn to live with. Yet the matter can be taken further than that.

One side of this duality, the side of both participation and service, of fulfillment of self in social life and of loyalty with all in pursuit of a common mission, is itself in a condition of tension. For the reasons just cited, no complete resolution of even this secondary tension can be expected. But by knowing the nature of the occupations which give rise to this tension, we can know at least that the tension is a genuine one, and that in itself will be helpful. Further, by reflecting upon the occupations involved, we can see that from the point of view of our democratic values this tension has a utility of its own. We should object to having it eliminated by the amputation of one or another of its parts. As democrats, we do not wish our citizens to serve loyally with a mere obsequious servility. We wish them to serve, but to serve proudly. We wish them to participate. On the other hand, we expect more from our citizens than merely formal participation. We demand loyal participation. We have come to this state by defining the mission in which we all must loyally serve as consisting, in part, in the establishment of a community within which all participate after the pattern of the Periclean Ideal. That ideal is not merely ours. We have solemnly, however tacitly, covenanted together in our history to establish that ideal as a practical reality. It will be dangerous if we fail to realize that in doing this we have conjoined two divergent ethical systems, two divergent ethical attitudes.

Much the same kind of observations can be made about the major tension in our inherited conception of citizenship. If we know the nature of the occupations which occasion the division between public and private in our citizenship, we can know that this division is, indeed, a tension and not the result of flat contradiction. Certainly, there is a tendency for the private occupation to imply complete withdrawal from civic concerns. Certainly, there is a tendency to put the requirements of private purpose ahead of public need and to justify this on the highest of moral grounds. Yet, in so far as the private occupation retains a Christian character of some completeness, there is an assurance that social awareness will not be wholly obscured. In that religion, there are two great commandments, not just one. Much more important, if we are aware of the kind of person who was expected to undertake the private occupation as it was defined in our history, then we will be that much more aware of the kind of person the citizen will be from whom we expect participation and loyalty. We will be that much more aware, in fact, of the kind of participation and loyalty we expect from him. Because of the nature of his private occupation, he will bring to his social involvements an understanding of his own individuality, of his ultimate responsibility for his own acts. He will insist upon recognition of, and respect for, the uniqueness of his own personality and he will be ready to grant the same recognition and respect to his fellows. He will resist all total involvements, for as he is a citizen here, so he is also a citizen elsewhere. He will hold, in short, to the duality of his citizenship—and all that that implies.

All of this should appear to be useful information and observation. There is only one serious difficulty with it: it is based exclusively on a genetic account of ideas which have been no more than asserted to be all within the modern concept of citizenship. The account has been historical, however philosophical the reflections. But no account has been given of how, or when, the three aspects of citizenship came together in the modern concept. It was suggested that Roman citizenship retained, as a secondary citizenship, something of the Greek meaning of the term. But Roman citizenship, in the account so far given, was supposed to comprise only one part of one of citizenship's three major meanings. An attempt was made in the introductory chapter to show that all three of these ideas are now involved in the modern notion of citizenship, but the analysis was semantic and was only suggestive. To demonstrate conclusively that these ideas are now combined in the modern concept of citizenship would require very nearly a full history of Western political thought. But, though the account so far has been in the main historical, the purpose has not been even to begin a history of this sort.

Something will be done, however, to make a little more convincing the assertion that these three ideas, so far described only in their original settings, do in fact now comprise the meaning of modern citizenship. I intend in the following chapters to discuss some of the philosophic problems which our present commitment to these ideas occasions. It will be useful to that enterprise to present first some material illustrative—though no more than illustrative—of the form which these ideas have taken in the modern American environment. This material will also go some way to confirm that these ancient ideas not only have been brought down to present times, but also have been specifically included within modern notions of citizenship.

In all this, however, I admit to no illusions about what I am doing and am asking my reader to do along with me. I have pointed to certain value patterns arising, roughly, one, two, and three thousand years ago. I now wish to go on to insist that these value patterns are poorly understood and badly defended in the more widely current social philosophies, and that therefore modern philosophers must boldly set about working up new concepts and arguments to do the job. The assumption throughout is not merely that there is in Western history a causal connection between, on one hand, the ancient facts that the Greeks, Hebrews, and Christian-Romans each cherished certain values and, on the other hand, the modern fact that we now hold very similar values. The assumption is further that because there is this causal connection we ought to be, indeed must be, much concerned to ensure that the ancient values are not lost from sight or otherwise neglected in the confusions of modern life. As a "traditionalist," I rest my argument squarely on the proposition that this historical connection between ancient and modern exists and that it is this connection which has determined both what we, in our citizenship, are and what we ought to be. Without this connection there would be no point either in deploring, as I will, John Stuart Mill's failure to understand and defend the ancient values or in attempting, as I also will, to erect conceptual schemes by which these values can be expressed more clearly and more firmly.

I cannot, in a book whose primary purpose is philosophical, do more than establish the existence in our history of certain patterns of ideas. This I think I have done. To establish the connection between these patterns and our own modern ways of thinking, I must rely upon the general agreement that Western thought displays in its history a remarkable continuity and consistency. More specifically, I can point to the fact that the works of Plato and Aristotle, of the Hebrew prophets and the Gospel writers, of Cicero, Paul, and Augustine have been constant and significant influences in Western thought. I have been mainly dependent upon the works of these men and, as it happens, all of them wrote as much for our age as they did for their own, however much their thought must be and has often been understood afresh. Beyond this I cannot do more. I turn immediately to see what form the idea patterns which these men helped to create have taken in the modern, especially the American, environment.

American allegiance to the ideal of civic participation can be quickly illustrated. The New England town meeting is dear to the hearts of the writers of our textbooks because of its mere existence. The question whether it is an effective governmental institution seems to be a quite separate matter. For illustrative purposes, not much more needs to be said. The American attitude toward politics is, as it is in so many things, ambivalent. Politics is to be used as a source of handouts to special interests. Politics is to be blissfully ignored and, failing that, despised. But politics, in America, is as frequently idealized, and it is only to this last facet of popular attitudes that I am concerned at the moment to point. It would be hard to say whether the political life was more idealized in some of the sentiment surrounding the Revolution and a few of the first state governments than it is in our numerous modern schools of citizenship. The idealization seems to have been a relatively constant source of inspiration, even if only intermittently applied. Sometimes it was expressed in attempts to reform formal political institutions, as in the fervor once displayed for such things as the referendum, the initiative, and the recall. There, Americans wanted not only democracy but Pure Democracy. More often it is displayed in the truly righteous enthusiasm for the politics of charity, fraternal club, church, school, and volunteer fire department. The unjoined American, it would appear, is an un-American American. Immorally, he is not participating in the life of his community, is not fulfilling his *telos* as a social being. At least this is partially true, perhaps one third true.

The presence in the American tradition of the notion of the loyal citizen is also easily illustrated. This notion requires two things: first, a sense of national community and, together with that, a sense of a national destiny in the pursuit of which citizens can be morally compelled to assist. It may be unusual but it is not strange that it was the second of these which arrived first on our shores. The Pilgrim Fathers and the first Virginian settlers did not share with each other a communal sense, but both groups did possess a conviction that they, each group in its own way, were establishing in this virgin land a New Israel, that they were making a new beginning which would, when completed, stand as a compelling and corrective challenge to the old and bad left behind. What was true of these first groups was true of a large proportion of those who came later. It was particularly true of all the thousands of little people (not excepting the Scotch-Irish) who struggled overseas and then on back to the Western frontier in the hope of opportunity, however variously defined. They did not come merely to settle: they came to build, to fashion a new world if only for themselves.

The sense of nationhood did not solidify until much later. It was still woefully weak at the time of the Revolution, and some historians do not count upon it as a solid and determining force in American life until after the War of 1812. But the sense of the new land's mission in the world was a constant encouragement to the formation of nationhood and with Lincoln, Unionist above all else, the notions of nation and national destiny were joined classically and finally:

. . . our fathers brought forth on this continent a new nation, conceived in liberty, and dedicated to the proposition that all men are created equal. Now we are engaged in a great civil war, testing whether that nation, or any nation so conceived and so dedicated, can long endure.[1]

Since then, the development of these notions has burgeoned. The sense of the oneness of the national community is never questioned. The definition of the national mission has hardly changed, though the techniques of its pursuit and the language used to express it have changed greatly. The chauvinistic bravado of the 1890's has given way first to the, in retrospect, blissful idealism of World War I and this in turn to the more prosaic idealism of the Atlantic Charter. The current situation finds our idealism much sobered though our passions are not. We are far more realistic than formerly about what we can do, but in that realism is contained the knowledge, new and not a little terrifying, of America's responsibilities as champion of the free world. We live in a world in which anxiety is routine and no one suggests taking on more ideals than we must. But this is not to say that nationhood and national destiny demand any less loyalty. On the contrary, as we all know, the demands for service are harsher and more inclusive than ever before. But again this is only part of the story, even though, in recent years, it has seemed to be the major portion of it.

Americans, pre-eminently, have been known as individualists. Since the days of Citizen Tom Paine, this has been the first value of their citizenship. Individualism came to America primarily because the forces which recreated and re-expressed it in Europe at the beginning of the modern age were the same forces which forced the breakout of the West from Europe. These forces are identified by historians as the Renaissance, the Reformation, and the rise of the bourgeoisie, although the labels tend to fragmentize what is often better viewed as a single movement. The complex spirit of that movement, together with the rather literal notions of democracy to which it gave rise, penetrated deeply into the traders, adventurers, Protestants, and those simply wanting "a new start" who came to America. They were all individualists—at least to the extent of having come to the point of considering their private interests and destinies more important than the collective welfare of the communities which they left behind. And all that individualism, once on the American "frontier," not only in the sense of an actual western frontier but also in the sense applicable to a new, rapidly developing community, was put on its mettle.

The early articulation of individualism in America can be noticed in three different areas. There is, first, the middle-class morality associated with the homilies of Ben Franklin and with the proverbial practices of the Yankee (Puritan) traders. There are, second, the beliefs of the American representatives of the Enlightenment about rational man capable of self-perfection if only given the requisite opportunities. There is, finally, what was later but much more sweeping, the spiritual individualism of Evangelical Protestantism.

These three strands combined to express *American* individualism, something quite different from the individualism then developing in Europe. There, individualism was a protest, but in America, individualism was largely isolated from the opposition. It was simply the American way. On its negative side, it insisted, loudly when necessary, on the brute claim of simply "let me alone"; on its positive side, it ascribed to the individual all the spiritual authority necessary for his coming to terms with God—whoever and whatever "god" might be—and assumed him to be in possession of all talents necessary for his advancement in this world. If he did not get on, that was his own affair. The fault was probably moral debility. These doctrines were imbued with the confidence and hope characteristic of "frontier" life. They were held with that common-sense self-assurance typical of those who are aware of only one side of a question. The result was an individualism far more wide-sweeping, far more immune to interference and attack, far more liberating than anything European liberals could incorporate within their thinking.

The unanimity with which the early Americans accepted this individualism—in the sense that even if few could express it, nearly all lived it—had important consequences. It made it easy for the philosophically inclined to utilize without qualm the contract theory of government —a theory which, from the very nature of contracts, emphasized not only individual consent but also the idea that individuals submitted to the rigors of government merely out of consideration for private interests. It prompted profound men to design a constitution in large part on the premise that men are motivated primarily by selfish interests and that, therefore, a first object in setting up a national government was to construct a legal environment within which conflicting private interests would battle each other to a salutary stalemate.

Among the numerous advantages promised by a well-constructed Union, none deserves to be more accurately developed than its tendency to break and control the violence of faction. . . . By a faction, I understand a number of citizens, whether amounting to a majority or minority of the whole, who are united and actuated by some common impulse of passion, or interest, adverse to the rights of other citizens, or to the permanent and aggregate interest of the community. . . . the *causes* of faction cannot be removed, . . . relief is only to be sought in the means of controlling its effects. . . . By what means is this object obtainable? . . . Either the existence of the same passion or interest in a majority at the same time must be prevented, or the majority, having such co-existent passion or interest, must be rendered, by their number and local situation, unable to concert and carry into effect schemes of oppression.[2]

Early American individualism also prompted the popular demand that a bill of rights be appended to the fundamental law of the land. Most of those rights were rights *against* the government, guarantees of a man's freedom to go his own way. They were stated in absolute terms: "Congress shall make no law . . . ," none whatsover. This kind of talk is to invite anarchy in wide areas of social life. But that is just what we must suppose the early Americans did want: as much anarchy as possible.

This was hardly a very sophisticated individualism. It talked almost exclusively in terms of passionate demands for freedom, for rights, and very little in terms of justifications, and not at all in terms which showed much awareness of the social context within which individuals always exist. Much has happened since those early, halcyon days to restrict it, even, many would say, to corrode it. The frontier is gone. It is gone long since in the sense of the Frontier of the West and the nativistic democracy which it almost directly created. It is also gone in the sense used to include the experience of the Andrew Carnegies and Henry Fords who, starting from scratch, became the proprietors of industrial empires created by themselves and in their own lifetimes. The frontier has been replaced by one, national, internally developing, socioeconomic monolith within which government, for example, is best viewed, for many purposes, as simply the largest single unit. It is true, beyond question, that America still displays a wonderful social mobility. But the up and coming do not rise to commands that they themselves have created. They rise from and through the ranks already there.

The existence now in America of a social, political, and economic order as enduring beyond private ambitions and as demanding of private concerns as any of the old orders left behind in Europe by the early Americans is readily apparent. So, too, are the major causes which created it. Big Society and Big Government are the consequences of total wars and very nearly total depressions; of the development of techniques of production and distribution demanding and creating an incredible degree of complexity and interrelatedness; of the creation of great strength, through industrialization, immigration, a rising standard of living, and the like, within an ever more confining space; of the creation of great wealth in an age which increasingly insists that all should have an equitable share of the benefits; of the total disappearance of a sense of military security, once lent by isolation and the British Navy, with the result that we live in what is sometimes called, aptly, a "garrison state." All of these causes, and many more not mentioned, appear to be more or less permanent features of our modern life. So also will be their consequences. The prospect before the American individualist, of his being able to preserve that aspect of his citizenship which, traditionally, he most dearly cherishes, is not a happy one.

Where can he look for assistance? He needs in the first instance to discover with precision the extent to which the scope for his individualism has been narrowed, the extent to which the legal and social barriers which used to defend it have given way, the extent to which, for example, that famous clause of the Fifth Amendment guaranteeing freedom from self-incrimination has been transformed from a right unquestioned into a stigma of shame. These almost statistical facts are being discovered by long-established organizations, by sympathetic foundations, by friendly newspapers, and even by, in the course of partisan strife, senatorial investigating committees. But, for intelligent men, to know these facts, to have them known widely through ingenious popularization, is only half the battle. Disturbing problems remain. Some of them, however important, are primarily practical such as the necessity of devising an internal security system which will do a job all admit must be done. Others, just as important in the long run, are more appropriate for philosophical texts: What place can individualism have in a modern democracy and what kind of individualism can it be? And further, how can it be defended, how can it be justified?

Answers to these latter questions will be attempted here. In our current situation, there is little need for a philosophic exposition of the ideals of civic participation, however much preaching of it may be necessary. Nor is there much need for a philosophic exposition of the loyalty aspect of citizenship—though there is much need for clarification of the mission, and its techniques—to which we and our country are called. But the philosophic condition of that part of our citizenship which means individualism is another matter. There the defenses are down. Worse, modern individualism is itself in a sorry state, incapable of much self-understanding or of hard thought for self-justification.

The basic pattern of Western individualism was described in Chapter III as possessing two parts. The first was a theory of dual citizenship. This theory gave to the second part, the notion of a private occupation, a social context. The notion of the private occupation was necessary, for otherwise individualism would have become vague, ultimately meaningless, and without purpose. But the social context, particularly in the form of a dual citizenship theory, was also necessary. The ancillary citizenship, that allowing membership in a particular society, was necessary to prevent the withdrawal which private occupation otherwise implied, while the higher citizenship was necessary for defending the private occupation on grounds other than that of selfish interpretation of private need. Together the two citizenships ensured a cleavage between a man and his particular community in terms of which he could, at once, admit and fulfill his social responsibilities and yet still preserve his individuality. In modern America both sides of this inherited pattern of individualism have withered. We say that we believe in the Bill of Rights but not only would we find it difficult to erect a universalized justification of it; we would find it nearly impossible to draw a clear-cut and convincing description of the private life which these rights are supposed to defend.

The withering of American convictions about the theory of dual citizenship is shown in many ways and has, no doubt, as many causes. Certainly the growth of nationalism has had much to do with it. The great mission which consumes our attention is not one concerned with the fate of some great society, greater than our own, whether it be the original Christian Brotherhood of Man or a more secular version of the same, the society of all humanity. Rather the great mission, the one which now claims all our efforts and which purports to be able to justify all such service as we do render, is the destiny which our own country must meet. In fact, the whole vision of a community morally greater and morally more significant than our own, bound by a Law whose divine inspiration was a measure of its moral superiority to our own mere human law, has faded perceptibly. Tom Paine had such a vision and his writings could both enrage and influence his times. Could they have a similar effect on our times?

At the risk of considerable misunderstanding, it can be suggested that the steady rise in the moral respectability of nationalism, our own at least, is itself but symptomatic of a general decline in "otherworldliness." It can be argued, therefore, that the abandonment of notions about a higher society in which we all are citizens should be viewed as a noticeable characteristic of modern culture. None of this should imply that Americans are less religious than they used to be. If anything, it must be suspected that they are more religious than Americans of fifty or a hundred years ago, both in the sense that modern Americans seem to be going to church in greater numbers and in the sense that they seem to be more responsive to religiously oriented appeals to morality. This may be asserted even in the face of the abundant evidence of "the pragmatic culture" and the extent to which modern psychology has morally debased "guilt" by reducing it to "guilt feeling." John Dewey, as a man and as a humanitarian, if not as a philosopher, can only be fully understood in terms of the religiously committed personality, in terms of a man religiously dedicated to the liberation of the human spirit.

What does seem to have happened is that Americans, whether religious in orthodox ways or not, have overwhelmingly gone over to the spirit of humanism. When "the fundamental problems of life" are faced, the maxims and ideals are formulated with far more reference than formerly to this world and this society. To call this merely the rise of secularism or materialism is to misunderstand modern America. There is still idealism; there is still a vision of a perfect society. But the perfect society is not one of which our present society is an imperfect imitation. Rather, the perfect society is no more than our present society improved to the point of perfection. The idealism can be and often is religious in a most profound sense. But the idealism is not about God and man (individually) so much as it is about man and God's work in this world. The world to come is the society of our children's children. Americans are now socially conscious in a way and to a degree they never were before. There is little room in their thoughts for that "other" society, the membership of which was once a prime support for an individualism still cherished if in name alone.

This same social consciousness, and the humanism of which it is an expression, has tended to obscure the notion of a private occupation, the notion that lies at the heart of traditional individualism. There is still, of course, some acceptance of the idea that you and I should stand aside, even at some expense to ourselves, in order to let a man work out his own fate. This is accepted, even if only partially, not on the grounds that his working it out for himself will be better for us and our society but simply on the grounds that it will be better for him. But the moral privilege of private occupation privately pursued for private gain (variously defined) has nowhere near the prestige it once possessed.

The arguments of recent years about the merits of "private enterprise" afford an example of this fact which not only illustrates it but typifies it generously. When the theories of capitalism, and of the liberalism with which it was for so long intimately associated, were first formulated, there was the underlying premise that man was solely motivated, for all practical purposes, by the desire for private profit. In the language of the economists, man was a rational creature whose first object was to equalize the marginal satisfactions to be derived from every alternative use to which his money could be put. For the Middle Ages this was the sin of avarice, but it constituted a base for a definition of a private occupation. The outward or social consequences of economic acts were, of course, of great importance, particularly to the first advocates of capitalism such as Adam Smith. But the inward consequences, the satisfactions which a man derived from his economic acts, always an integral part of the philosophy, were increasingly brought into view and were increasingly emphasized. Economic man was a doer, and more and more significance was attached to what he did and why. Less and less significance was attached to the resultant social consequences. Capitalism became a theory of private occupation in the hands of the men who ran industry in the nineteenth century. Nowhere was this more true than in America. Bourgeois ethics and Protestant, particularly Calvinist, ethics became as one. The virtues of thrift, hard work, and willingness to shoulder responsibility, the primary virtue of self-reliance, brought not only financial success. More important, the financial success was accepted as proof that all these virtues were possessed, and as tangible evidence of election by God. Later the influence of Darwinian theories about survival gave to these views a fashionable "realism" but did not even begin to eliminate the essentially religious conviction that the freedom of the market place was chiefly valuable as providing opportunity for each man to test the moral fiber of his soul. Money was success, but this was no crass materialism, for success was a victory of the spirit.

In every store and factory there is a constant weeding-out process going on. The employer is constantly sending away "help" that have shown their incapacity to further the interests of the business, and others are being taken on. No matter how good times are, this sorting continues, only if times are hard and work is scarce, the sorting is done finer—but out and forever out, the incompetent and unworthy go. It is the survival of the fittest. Self-interest prompts every employer to keep the best— those who carry a message to Garcia.[3]

It is hard for the present generation to understand how strongly these views were held considerably less than a hundred years ago. A reading now of Andrew Carnegie's speeches and essays leaves one gasping at what now appears to be either incredibly smug or incredibly ingenuous. Such has been the shift not only in the degree of our awareness of the consequences of unchecked capitalism but also in our attitudes about the spiritual therapy of "making money." The change has been swift but it has not been either abrupt or complete. Wilson's "New Freedom" speeches reveal how early and how sharp the awareness was of the consequences to ordinary men of the free enterprise of the few. But the notion that all must be allowed to compete was retained in full fervor. The logical implication of this notion, that the freely competitive economy must be preserved but without the spoils of victory being allowed to accrue to those who competed best, was not thought odd. Man's private occupation was still thought to be the trying of souls in the market place. By the time of the Roosevelt era, the ground had shifted again and now more drastically. The Great Depression made the consequences, in this case the failures, of capitalism too obvious and of too immediate concern to too many for the debate about its merits to take place on any other plane than the pragmatic one. The rich, the successful, and others who still cherished capitalism for the moral values inherent in its individualism simply could not get a hearing. They could only fume with moral indignation as the argument shifted steadily to the grounds which judged capitalism primarily on its social and material utility. That is still very largely the position today. Capitalism, by producing more bathtubs, telephones, automobiles than any system of socialism, makes free men wealthier. The argument that it might make them individually and internally spiritually healthier has been almost completely, even if not quite, forgotten. Humanism and social awareness are victorious— in all ranks of society, rich and poor, conservative and liberal alike.

Do we cheer? Do not we agree that the idea of private enterprise in the market place constituting a genuinely private occupation was always a myth and that, in a complex industrial community, it became a farce? And is it not true that capitalism produces more bathtubs, telephones, automobiles than any socialism yet tried? Is there anything wrong with social awareness, with being concerned with the material welfare of our fellow men? I neither cheer nor weep, at least not in the present connection. I am merely concerned to point out that in the modern defense of capitalism, social utility is of far more importance than private utility. In this respect, the modern defense of capitalism is characteristic of our age. Private occupation has lost its status of moral privilege. Not just private enterprise, but all occupations, however personally satisfying, are ultimately justifiable only on grounds of public utility. All rights, all loyalties, all participation are good, but only in so far as they meet and advance the public convenience. Private need for private occupation alone no longer justifies. There was no need for the Great Depression to demonstrate that private occupation has public consequences, however dramatically it brought home the point. No matter how defined, private occupation will always occasion some public effect. If I go off to my cave in the mountains to starve in inner contemplation of my god, I am reducing the number of the able-bodied available for the defense of my community. But there was a time when the tension between public and private could be maintained. There was a time when the interference in public life caused by private occupation could be defended from positions which could, on roughly equal terms, compete with those proclaiming the virtues of loyalty and participation. But this does not any longer seem to be the case.

It is not being contended that Americans are no longer individualists. So far as general spirit and feeling go, they are as unquestionably individualistic as any modern people. But it is being contended that they no longer know what they wish to be individuals *for,* and, lacking this knowledge, they crave freedom only to be publicly useful. The anonymous work of the soul no longer satisfies. We must be known and our work widely known. Then we are somebody. Unknowns are nobodies. Those who are not "important," somehow and to some community, hardly have a claim to existence. "Togetherness" is the accepted ideal in the nursery, and in commercial, political, and intellectual activities the "team" is the accepted instrument of progress. It is not just a question of justification by works. The works must be part of the group activity and, in the end, be seen to advance the interest of the group. It makes little difference whether the group is family, party, corporation, or country, or whether "my group" is in conflict or competition with others. Acceptance by and contribution to the group are all that count. And with the lack of thought for even the possibility of a private occupation within, beyond, or outside the group has gone also both the desire for and the vision of a higher community in which, as strangers, we could all be citizens. The only community that matters is the present community. In fact, in terms of ultimate bases for convincing moral justifications, that community made up of my present peers is all that matters. I must adjust to it, for the maladjusted individual is neurotic. I must participate in that community's civic life. I must be loyal and serve in its communal mission. But I may not, it often seems, have a life apart from it. The first virtue is to be agreeable and sincerely so. The first sin is to be divisive, a cause of controversy. There is no room any more for the indifferent man. There is hardly room for the social critic—except on society's own terms. I am not a man. I am an American. In today's society, how terribly pretentious—and yet how nostalgically familiar—seem the words of Thoreau: ". . . any man more right than his neighbors constitutes a majority of one already." [4]

From the point of view of the traditional form of individualism, this is an unhappy situation and it is made no happier by the philosophies to which Americans on occasion turn for exposition and defense of their individualism. In political philosophy, Americans are both singularly unoriginal and undiverse. There are only two defenses of freedom which count for much in the popular American mind. One is the language of the Bill of Rights and the Declaration of Independence. The other is John Stuart Mill's essay *On Liberty*. "I have my rights" and "I ought to be free so far as I don't harm others," are the two classic statements by which Americans defend their rights to be let alone. Both are expressions of philosophies which are either so woefully inappropriate or so woefully confused that neither is capable, except by tour de force, of defending or justifying freedom, particularly private freedom for private purpose, in a modern environment.

It may well be necessary to make very clear that, in terms of fundamentals, I have no quarrel to pick either with Mill's essay or, on the other hand, with the Declaration of Independence and the Bill of Rights. All three of these documents are evidence of basic value commitments which I would be the first to applaud and which I would insist I share. And I know full well that these documents have become, quite properly, symbols in the cause of freedom. As such, they have an important fighting value. My quarrel is not with these documents as documents. My quarrel is with the philosophies which these documents use to express the values we all share. Those philosophies, I insist and will try to show, simply do not and cannot do the job. If we take them seriously, I think it can be seen that not only do they fail to express and defend our values. I think it can also be seen that they tend to confuse us and, worse, actually mislead us as to what it is that in these trying times we should most eagerly defend.

It is the philosophy behind the Bill of Rights and the Declaration of Independence which is inappropriate to modern conditions. It is so because that philosophy was part and parcel of a general world view which commands little general acceptance today. The Declaration, the Bill of Rights, and the Constitution itself were all the work of men filled with the outlook of the Enlightenment. The philosophy of the Enlightenment is often identified in general as Deism, which is accurate enough, but it is more descriptive to call it a thoroughgoing Rationalism which saw man as Reason, the world as rationally ordered, and man's life in the world as an adventure which, by due application of rational intelligence, could top the heights of perfect reasonableness. The ethics were as certain, self-assured, and optimistic as Newtonian physics, for both were parts of the same outlook. This outlook was dominant in America for a brief but critical period. The men who managed the Revolution and were responsible for the establishment of the young nation believed it, even if the mass of the population had no comprehension of it. But Deistic Rationalism had no great hold in America, and it was soon replaced by more orthodox views, mainly theological. In so far as these have been replaced in turn, they have been replaced first by Idealism, then by Darwinism, and finally by the various versions of modern empiricism. Yet Deistic Rationalism did succeed in getting itself written into our basic documents. These are much revered and because of that we have the somewhat absurd situation in which, while very few indeed any longer believe in Natural Law in the way that either Jefferson or Madison believed in it, very many talk much about our Natural or, sometimes, our Inherent Rights.

There is a certain absurdity in even the very notion that a modern, complex, tense yet hopefully democratic community should persist in talking the language of Natural Rights. Such a language may be appropriate for describing, even proclaiming, a situation in which broad freedom exists for all men almost as a bounty of nature. But it is singularly inappropriate for a situation in which only a small measure of individual freedom can be carved out of our vast social monolith and even that only with much pain, perseverance, and ingenuity. In such a situation, the first object must be the condition of freedom itself. The rights which are to secure that freedom should, in all intelligence, be just those which are expressly designed for the freedom desired. These rights must be designed, too, with full awareness of the social situation within which such freedom as can be allowed must inevitably exist.

But the doctrine of Natural Rights allows no such flexibility. The rights desired are stated in absolute terms and, worse, many of them are named as if for all time and all circumstances, even if the names given are mostly not susceptible of precise definitions. What then happens in practice is that these absolute and named rights, though still, of course, asserted absolute, are qualified, as they must necessarily be, on every turn. The principles by which they are qualified cannot be stated, for the absolute is not qualifiable. Attempts to state such principles never succeed in doing more than simply removing the problem from one area to another. We have freedom of speech, absolutely, but if our exercise of it presents a "clear and present danger," then it may be abridged. The question then is not only when is danger clear and present and who is to decide if that point has been reached. The major question remains: What is dangerous? Does not all this, in any case, somehow imply that we have a Natural Right to be *non*-dangerous? The attempt to define and qualify one Natural Right has resulted in the spawning of another, just as undefinable as anything before. "Heresy, yes, but conspiracy, no," says, quite remarkably, a modern empiricist. But, to be rude, which is which? That matter, apparently, must be left to common sense.

These defects in the doctrine of Natural Rights have a quite obvious source in the philosophy of which that doctrine was a part. The Enlightenment philosophers thought of rights as inhering in man immediately. They could not conceive, because their philosophy would not allow them to conceptualize, rights coming to a man through public grant by society. The phrase in the Declaration of Independence which asserts that man has "these rights" by an act of divine "endowment" is no more than a figure of speech. What it meant to convey, as in the philosophy of Locke, was that these rights belonged to man directly; they were his by the very nature of man as created. Government's only role could be to "protect" each man in his possession of them. This view made the doctrine incurably blind. It could never learn that rights, to be possessed in any meaningful way, must be granted by a society and its government to individuals. Rights, as will be suggested at greater length in the next chapter, are only meaningful as social institutions, as ways of doing things in society. For a society and its government to grant rights, they must be persuaded that certain things, which they admit ought to be done, can be best done by granting those rights.

But the doctrine of Natural Rights could not allow any such debate. All attention was concentrated on the rights alone, the rights to life, to liberty, and to the pursuit of "happiness." There was no definition of the ends for the accomplishment of which the rights might be the means. No justification was offered for possession of the rights. None was needed, because, by this doctrine, they were already "possessed."

Furthermore, argument about why rights should be possessed was also precluded because, by understanding man to have rights, whether in a "State of Nature" or in a commonwealth, whether in or out of a society, man was seen as complete in himself. Government was no more than a "convenience," and society, that social context without which man, on most views, can hardly be conceived to be man at all, had, in the philosophy of Natural Rights, no significant existence. There could be no debate about rights because not only was there nothing to debate about; there also did not appear to be anything with which to debate. There could be no question about modifying the rights, qualifying them, adapting them because society and *its* needs, which might demand the modification, qualification, and adaptation, were not known and could not be understood to exist. In the language of citizenship evolved in earlier chapters, the philosophy of Natural Rights conceived all occupations to be private. Its claims, therefore, came down to no more than the flat assertion "I have my rights"—an assertion which would brook no argument and which would offer no definitions. And it made this assertion in happy innocence of all the hard questions which plague the modern citizen who exists, and is regularly reminded that he exists, within the confining context of society.

One cannot help envying the simplicity of the doctrine of Natural Rights. Its claims do have a certain noble ring. This is even more true of that literary masterpiece, Mill's essay *On Liberty*. Nowhere have the claims of freedom been stated in more moving terms. And the influence of this essay in the United States has been so great that it has become, to all intents, part of the orthodox American heritage, in large part because Mill did see that what the individual must fear most is not Government, but rather is that public opinion which, in a democracy, particularly a mass democracy, governments are increasingly prone to follow rather than lead. Mill wanted "an *atmosphere* of freedom" and in this he was right in a way which only a modern citizen can know. But beyond this, Mill's merits in the essay

On Liberty are chiefly literary. Philosophically, even merely logically, confusion abounds. His thesis, that I should be free in so far as I do not harm others, does not help in the solution of disputes. It only multiplies them.

The fact that Mill often posed as a thoroughgoing Utilitarian and yet frequently opposed Utilitarianism's basic concepts in most alarming ways is not of direct concern here. The essay is accepted for its defense of liberty, and it is primarily the modern American acceptance of that defense as adequate which creates problems for us. Mill's later revisions of his own thinking have not lessened the popularity of the essay as written in the least. And his occasional flat contradiction in it of his inheritance, and therefore of himself, if anything makes his defense of freedom all the more acceptable. Self-contradiction, apparently, sometimes improves plausibility.

The only contradictions with which we are concerned are those which arise from Mill's attempt to define, and then prove legitimate, certain limitations upon the activity of the state and society. His general statement of the problem makes it clear that his first interest in this essay is only to state the case for the liberty of the individual from "compulsion" whether by "legal penalties or the moral coercion of public opinion." This is in itself an unhappy beginning. In modern society, the case for freedom from "compulsion" cannot be fully put without considerable reference to that other freedom, sometimes called "positive freedom" or "freedom *for*," which views the society and the state as morally obligated to restrict freedom in the usual sense in order to increase, by various means, the freedom or capacity of individual citizens to live happily, intelligently, and morally. The modern society is not only concerned that its citizens be free to come and go and do in some measure as they please; the modern society is also concerned to ensure, *by compulsion if necessary,* that all its citizens receive, for example, something of an education. There are few considerations of this sort in Mill's essay. In fact, the conclusion at which he finally arrives, that the sole warrant for compulsion by state or society is to prevent "harm," seems to forbid the consideration of compulsion for welfare at all. This defect not only dates Mill badly; it grievously inhibits his argument.

Much the same point can be put in another and perhaps more dramatic way. Mill's basic statement of the problem takes too much the form of only "Individual *vs.* the Community." This is doubly unfortunate. *Liberté, Égalité,* and *Fraternité* are *all* parts of the democrat's creed. They are all necessary to him and they all more or less contradict each other. The democrat's task is to maintain a tense balance between the three. Mill's fault was not only misplacement of too great emphasis. It was also that he seemed to think he could discuss *Liberté* without equally discussing *Égalité,* and *Fraternité.* To put the problem so much in the form of "Individual *vs.* the Community" is unfortunate because it blinds both Mill and his casual reader to the fact that all liberties, whether for private or public purposes, whether from the state and social opinion or from other forces, are only to be had within the communal context. This is true in part because the state, unlike some of the voluntary groups within it, is an inclusive organization. It is also true from the very nature of man's social life. There can be a liberty from the state, if the state, in its might, allows it. But there can be no liberty *from* the community, only liberty *within* the community. That this is no mere matter of words will be seen more clearly as the argument develops.

The source of these preliminary and yet fundamental difficulties in Mill is very similar to the source of the inadequacy of the Natural Rights philosophy. Neither Mill nor the Natural Rights philosophers had, or could have had, a vigorous theory of society. (This is only one of a number of similarities between the two views, all of which Mill would have been loath to admit.) Mill had more reason to know, because he feared, the community. He knew there existed a sovereign majority in the democracies being established in his day, and he feared their mass mediocrity. He hastened to distinguish between the quality of the pleasures of the many and the quality of the pleasures of the few. But, as a philosopher, he could neither explain the community nor take account of it in his defense of that liberty from it which, as a gentleman and a scholar, he cherished so much. He was committed to an atomistic view of society by his father, the same view which all the Utilitarians inherited from Hobbes and Locke. Mill could not have escaped from it even had he wished to. As consequence, Mill's defense of liberty could only be of a liberty which cannot exist, a liberty *from* society. He could not defend that real liberty which we can enjoy, liberty within and created by our society.

Mill's actual defense of liberty is based on a distinction between public and private which purports to see some actions as private because they are only "self-regarding" and without effect upon anyone else, and other actions as public because they do affect other people. There can be grave doubt as to whether there are any significant actions which I can take which my neighbors might not be at least taught to consider as affecting them in one way or another. However this may be, the distinction in itself prompts Mill to put what is the first of three major arguments for personal freedom. State, community, and neighbors have no right to meddle in my private affairs because my private affairs are not (and cannot be, apparently) any of their business, and are of no concern (and, again, can be of no concern) to them. Taken literally, the advice is almost gratuitous, but the language is persuasive all the same.

Mill's next major argument on behalf of personal liberty —and this is the one for which his essay is chiefly famous— is that diversity, which only an atmosphere of freedom can create, is a good thing. The argument is applied primarily to the areas of thought and expression. In these areas, diversity, and all the argument which marks it, ensures that error will not long go undetected. Secondly, without diversity, much truth would never be discovered. And, finally, vigorous and sustained diveristy of opinion ensures that such truth as is discovered will be made to appear vital, interesting, even pleasant. There can be no disputing the force of these points, but the modern citizen may fail to be as impressed with them as Mill was. The argument is essentially practical in the sense that, given liberty, the truth will out. Over a period of time, that may be so, but we may not be able to wait. Put the other way around, knowing the efficacy of modern techniques of communication and advertising, the contemporary citizen may be inclined to agree with James Thurber's moral to the effect that, while you may not be able to fool all the people all the time, you can fool too many of them too much of the time. Even more serious is the question whether we can be sure that the truth which freedom's processes may bring will prove to be in our frail society both constructive and pleasant. Modern science has undoubtedly been bred in the tradition of free inquiry, of the pursuit of truth for truth's sake. Yet modern science has bequeathed us the automobile, the airplane, and the atom, none of which can be called unmixed blessings. A case of at least some persuasiveness can be made out to insist that man is not yet wise enough to be trusted (freely) with the truth that free-dom brings.

But much more important than these observations is the fact that, by advancing these arguments that freedom will bring truth, Mill has, for the moment, completely aban-doned his original position. He claimed that we should be free in all those areas in which our actions do not "affect" others. But he now argues that some of these "private" ac-tions do affect others, that the consequence of giving us liberty to undertake these actions privately will not only affect society but will be of immense public advantage. Later, Mill qualifies his meaning of "affect" with the con-clusion already mentioned that we should be free so long as we do not "harm" others. We should be free, presuma-bly, to produce good effects, that is, nonharmful ones. But even this qualification will not save the present argument. It may very well be to my interest to ensure that certain errors, in the beliefs, for example, that my neighbors may have about my private affairs, go undetected. Indeed, it may well be to my interest that certain truths about politics, religion, or morality are never discovered by the popular mind. Mill is saying, in effect, that all criticism must be "fair." But he surely must have known that criticism, partic-ularly the criticism which is so devastatingly put as to be really effective, will always be thought by some to be un-fair, that it will rarely be taken other than badly, especially by those who stand most in need of it.

Moreover, there is no advantage in sympathetically and most generously interpreting Mill's use of the word "affect" to mean that private actions are those for which I, on some undefined moral standard, should alone be held responsi-ble. Perhaps what Mill was trying to say was that, for ex-ample, I should be solely responsible for my own adult education but that I might legitimately be required to share responsibility with the community for the education of my children. We can, for the moment, disregard the fact that this interpretation of "affect" introduces a whole maze of new questions about the standards determining those things for which I alone should be responsible and on which Mill offers no guidance at all. But there remains the spectacle of Mill arguing that I alone should be responsible for my own thoughts and their expression, while he is at the same time demonstrating that the consequences of my being so allowed will be of genuine concern to society. Where there is genuine concern, so also is there genuine ground for responsibility. Mill's essential argument is that it would be imprudent for state or society to meddle in areas of thought and expression. This may or may not be so. But if it is, then it is because Mill has succeeded in proving to us that the community is affected, is concerned, and should, therefore, be responsible for "the truth" operative within its boundaries. Unavoidably and uncomfortably true as this may be, it is the last thing Mill would deliberately have set out to prove, because it raises questions and casts out implications on every side which Mill had neither the equipment nor the nerve to face.

The third major argument which Mill introduces in defense of personal liberty refers to "the intrinsic worth" of individuality. This argument has played only a minor role in bringing the essay fame, but it is certainly the one which adds most to the essay's stature. It has two sides. There is in Mill a strong, not altogether obvious yet easily discoverable, bias toward Aristotelian notions about self-fulfillment. Men must be allowed to grow. The other side of the argument appears more faintly but, knowing something of Mill, we can be sure that he held it as strongly as any other conviction. This asserts the absolute and sole responsibility of each man for his own moral welfare. You cannot make a man grow; you can only let him develop his own capacities. You, the state, the community are morally obligated to let man alone. It would be ignoble to meddle in his self-development.

It is well known that, as a Utilitarian, Mill had no right to introduce this argument. Yet this is of little consequence. Mill believed it fervently, and in that conviction he was as true to our Western heritage as any man. But it also must be at once obvious that these three major arguments in defense of liberty—that you cannot meddle in my private affairs because it is none of your business; that diversity is a good thing and that therefore it is imprudent to meddle; and that it is ignoble to meddle because of the intrinsic worth of the individual—are incompatible. It can scarcely be imagined that a man could fulfill himself by acting only in the sphere where his actions affected no one but himself. The ethical grounds of prudence are not only different from but contradictory to those which assert moral legitimacy absolutely. By arguing from the intrinsic worth of the individual, Mill comes remarkably close to asserting that it is from the very nature of man as man that the obligation to leave him to his own self-development springs. This is, or is at least a basis of, a doctrine of Natural Rights in all but name. It implies, probably correctly, that what Mill really wanted was a society in which, whether it seemed socially prudent or not, each man would be as free as humanly possible to pursue his own self-development. For this Mill should be applauded.

But we are still entitled to ask him heatedly what he then means by his final principle for determining the limits of the activity of the state. That principle, as he stated it, is

. . . the sole end for which mankind are warranted, individually or collectively, in interfering with the liberty of action of any of their number, is self-protection . . . is to prevent harm to others.[5]

What does he mean by "harm"? Does he not realize that for liberty, for a society in which men are genuinely free, we must pay a price? Is he not willing to admit that a truly free society, for all its legitimacy, will be dangerous, unstable, inefficient, and one in which men will be constantly liable to "harm" each other, particularly on their own definitions of "harm"?

Mill was incapable of realizing or admitting any of these things. His ultimate justification for liberty, the one which probably counted most with him, he had to mute not only because of his Utilitarianism, but also because he instinctively felt that freedom for "me" would have to be shown to be of practical use to the sovereign majority. His father and Bentham had enthroned that majority as sovereign in the cause of democracy. The younger Mill could not state fully his case for private freedom nor could he state, perhaps not even to himself, the implications of that case. To insist all the way upon the "intrinsic worth" of the individual would have implied at least a partial dethronement of the sovereign majority, would have implied that the sovereign majority must, whether it seemed wise or not, let the individual alone. It would have implied, in short, that the individual citizen, while a citizen here, had other occupations and other loyalties.

The basic criticism of Mill's essay remains. In it, Mill set out to defend private liberty and he had some idea of why that liberty was worth having. But his most impressive arguments do not defend that liberty. They defend rather the value of letting men be free to contribute to the public good. On the other hand, the liberty to contribute freely, to participate and serve—liberties which the democrat cherishes quite as much as any other type—Mill never identifies as worth defending. In this essay he bound himself too much to the notion that his problem was that of the one against the many. He did not set himself the task of finding a liberty for the one *among* the many and, in the end, he never succeeded in defending the right of the one to go his own way despite the interests of many. Such are the confusions in which in this essay Mill left the defense of liberty. Perhaps that is why his essay is popular: there is something in it for everybody. But confusion does not prove or justify anything. It only confuses, and the popularity of the essay *On Liberty* is a measure of the confusion which surrounds the defense of liberty today.

Mill's essay and the Natural Rights doctrine of the Declaration of Independence and the Bill of Rights are by no means the only defenses of liberty offered in the United States today. They are the most usual, and this to a very great extent. But there are others and some of these have, within certain narrow circles, a quite considerable popularity. It is strange that one of the best known of these somewhat esoteric defenses of freedom, that associated with John Dewey and his followers, persists in borrowing extensively from Mill's uncertain arsenal.

Before accusing this group of suffering from many of Mill's shortcomings, we should point out first that the Dewey school is considerably more agile and professional at the defense of liberty than Mill. The men of this school know their business and they are careful. They know with some clarity that what they want is a free *society*. They understand society as Mill never did. Furthermore, by equating freedom with the needs of the spirit of modern scientific tenchiques, they have given freedom an exactness of definition which it previously did not possess. These are real virtues. They have resulted in an important shift, at least of scholarly and professional opinion, away from a too narrow and vague concern for "my freedom." Attention is now directed to a more general concern for the precise conditions necessary for the "free society," for the wants of free men in what is sometimes graphically called the "open" or, even better, the "open-ended society."

But, great as these considerable advantages are, the defense of freedom offered by Dewey and his followers still suffers from serious defects. The members of this group have concentrated on man's intelligence. They can, in their empiricism, detect the existence of this faculty, as a faculty, in man, for the "evidence" of its existence is everywhere at hand in man's frequent solution of the problems posed for him by his experience. The task these philosophers then set themselves is the liberation of this capacity. They wish to free man of the deadening influence of obsolescent dogma, of all the restrictions, petty and great, imposed by state and culture, which inhibit men from solving problems on the basis of merit and evidence alone. They want men to be free in both mind and spirit, to be unrestricted and unencumbered, to meet the problems of human experience squarely on the grounds on which that experience presents them.

The difficulty in this noble view is its overwhelming focus of attention on man's intellectual productivity. Though they never have had the opportunity, and, being decent men, would certainly never take it were it presented, they conceivably could be brought to argue that minds which did not produce should be eliminated. For the trouble with intellectual productivity, like all forms of productivity, is that it can only be measured meaningfully, can only be appreciated and held significant, in social terms. And this logical tendency is reinforced by the practical tendency arising from the fact that Dewey and all his followers were and are humanists to the core. They value a man because of what he can contribute to the welfare of other men. Like Mill, they value freedom because freedom of thought and expression produces more reliable information than any other method yet tried. Like the modern free enterprise capitalist, they value the free market place of ideas because such a market place is more productive of what the people and society want than any controlled market place. As a result, the individuality of the single man, whose claims to be allowed to *do* must be satisfied whether or not his action is socially efficient or publicly prudent, whose claims for liberty must be met whether or not he can use that liberty wisely and productively, the individuality of *this* man is lost sight of.

But again, as with Mill, there is no mystery about why Dewey and his followers really value freedom. They are all, ultimately but passionately, committed to a love of the independent and creative human spirit. They value that spirit in itself. The work that it may do is not really valuable to them for its social consequences. Rather it is valuable simply as expression of that human spirit. But Dewey and his followers cannot, within the terms of their empirically oriented ethics—and metaphysics, though they scrupulously deny that they have any—find the means to give expression to their basic value commitment. The goods of this life, they everywhere insist, must and can only be defined in "natural" terms, that is, in scientifically detectable terms. But of what scientifically verifiable matter does the human spirit consist? The dimensions of their general philosophy allow them to talk at will and at length of the activity, the thinking, problem-solving creativity of the human spirit—but do not allow them to detect directly, to identify and discuss, to say nothing of holding inviolate, the human spirit in itself as an objective reality. As consequence, Dewey and his men have been forced to drag their valuation of that spirit along almost unconsciously. They expose it only when they are forced to turn and fight. Only then does their philosophy ring with a defiant individualism. Under more placid circumstances their writings suggest no higher ideal than a vision of the wholly cooperative group in which the individual's only liberty is the freedom to participate—and conform.

The Dewey school(s) of philosophy have had an enormous practical influence in American life for nearly fifty years. Yet this has primarily been because Dewey's disciples have been influential people, especially in the public school system. Dewey's *arguments* for freedom can hardly be said to have had the vogue that Mill's still have. Therefore, though philosophically they deserve more respect, Dewey's arguments for individual liberty cannot be afforded more space here. I have discussed them at all only because Dewey's failure to be explicit and complete about what democrats want freedom *for* seems to epitomize the general inability of Americans to justify their claims to the traditional rights.

This is the condition of the traditional philosophy of individualism in America today. There is no need to wonder, then, at the impervious effrontery of the poll takers when they ask us the most intimate personal questions. In the modern situation, with the notion of individualism so derelict, its defenses so weak, there can be no persuasive rebuttal to the poll takers' argument that the information they collect from us about our "private" lives may eventually be put to the good public use of, for example, saving marriages, or even sometimes, to judge by the questions asked, of defending freedom.

V

THE DEFENSE OF INDIVIDUALISM

IN MODERN SOCIETY

A very considerable audacity is required in any attempt to say something constructive about the condition of individ- · ualism in modern America. It might well be better to let the matter rest with what I have already tried to establish: that, traditionally, Western democratic citizenship is a complex concept including at least three distinct "occupations," and that of these three the most important one, individualism, is, in the present situation, in a weakened condition, barely understood and poorly defended. But to attempt no more than this would imply an admission that individualism today is, philosophically, a lost cause. It is not a lost cause. Yet any new defense of it must be broadly based and must admit that difficulties, both theoretical and practical, will always persist. We must admit that individualism is only one of our civic ideals, and we must admit also that in so far as we will be individualistic we can be that only within a confining social context. We can be private men only if we admit our public duties.

But in undertaking to defend such individualism as can exist in modern conditions I am anxious to reiterate one rather obvious point. I undertake this task as a philosopher, not as a practical politician. As such, I can properly say, for example, that I think modern individualists must find for themselves a private occupation; and I should attempt to define the essential characteristics which that occupation ought to have. But it does not seem to be my business here to try to say exactly what, in our current circumstances, that occupation should be. That is a matter of practical judgment and is to be settled by the practical politicians charged with the management of our society. It is the practical politicians—that is, all of us in our ordinary active capacities as citizens—who must defend and practice individualism. The hope of the philosophically inclined—that is, of all of us when we try to reflect upon ourselves and our problems—is that intelligence and understanding will make the tasks of defending and practicing our individualism both easier and surer of positive result. What, therefore, follows in the present chapter must perforce be abstract. It will have significance only as it is given application by those who, in practical situations, have the opportunity to do so. And that, I again insist, means all of us.

Because of the abstract character of the material I must present here, it is important to put in fairly precise outline what I will be trying to do. The first point to be made is that individualism will not be defended or understood simply by discussing at greater and greater length the nature of that individualism as such. That must be done to some extent, of course, and in the previous chapters, especially the historical ones, I have tried to spell out the form not only of our traditional individualism but also of our other social ideals. J. S. Mill did not do this kind of thing enough. He was never clear about what exactly it was that he was trying to defend. But he did realize, and here I must emulate his example, that no individualism will be understood or defended unless some attempt is also made to see it within the context in which it is to be practiced. As a result, the first of the major questions now confronting me concerns the nature of the context within which the democratic citizen must find the opportunities to fulfill the commitments which his traditions have placed upon him.

That context, as we all know only too well, is supplied by society and, within it, by the state. What, then, is the nature of the relationship between the citizen and the state? The citizen must seek to do all that his traditions direct, but surrounding him on every side is the state whose power, even in a democracy, to compel obedience to *its* law is very nearly unchallengeable. This is the first question dealt with by the present chapter. The conclusion arrived at is that the state, for all its power, indeed, if only because it is so powerful, must be viewed by the citizen as the *primary* agent for establishing the conditions within which he can undertake the occupations of his citizenship.

On traditional American views this conclusion is not very pleasing, but I believe that it is unavoidable. The next part of the chapter is an attempt to analyze what the state in its power can do for the citizen. This analysis leads to conclusions as unpleasant but just as unavoidable as the one just mentioned. The state can do a great deal for the citizen, probably much more than many Americans would care to admit, but, unfortunately, there are no principles arising directly out of the nature of the state which will exactly delimit or otherwise define its activities. What the state should do is a matter for the determination of practical judgment. Two things only are available to instruct the masters of the state: their knowledge of current circumstances and what is possible within them, and, second, their understanding of the ideals which the citizens must be enabled by the state to pursue. This conclusion is worked out by an analysis of the primary instruments available to the state. These are the obligations which the state can compel and the rights which it can allow. The analysis of these instruments of the state, especially that of the nature of rights, again challenges in a fundamental way a number of cherished American prejudices. But I am convinced that if our courts, for example, in their decisions on questions of civil rights, are to maintain the cause of democracy in a deliberate way, much of our old ways of looking at these matters will have to be abandoned.

Having examined the principal components of the social context and its state, viewed philosophically, I then attempt to see what place can be found in that context for traditional individualism. I find here in the first instance that, no matter what the cost, the state must find some room in the social context for the practice of individualism. Democracy's chief claim to respectability is not that it is efficient in the ordinary sense; the claim is that, whether efficient or not, democracy aims to be legitimate government. And there can be no legitimacy for a Western government without individualism. I then, after surveying again the nature of traditional individualism and stressing the importance of each of its aspects to democracy, turn to a general examination of what traditional individualism requires of us if we are to have it as a vital part of our modern way of life. The major conclusion here is that modern individualism will have to rely, much more than our current secularism might permit, upon the generality of our Christian heritage. Democracy, in sum, because of the individualism which is central to it, must be recognized as being as much a political theology as it is a political philosophy.

The development of the argument just outlined can best begin with a reminder of two of the basic conclusions which I have already arrived at about the nature of democratic citizenship. The most obvious of these, and yet the one most needing constant reiteration, is that all of the aspects of our citizenship must be given due emphasis. Not only that. We must remember, at whatever costs to consistency and logical neatness, that there are real tensions between the ideals of participation, service, and privacy. These tensions are not only inevitable but they are also useful and characteristic features of the democratic way of life. Citizenship in the Western tradition is not a simple thing, and all of its complexities must be kept in sight, however cumbersome and difficult this may be.

More positively, we must remember to emphasize, with all the vividness our imaginations can supply, that the citizen is an actor, a doer, a source of energy and activity. The citizen is not merely an object, to which rights and obligations adhere. Nor is citizenship any list of rights and obligations. The citizen acts, does, and pursues, and the meaning of citizenship can only be found in a description of the ideals and goals which should govern his activity. The equality of citizens, in the Western tradition, stems ultimately from this understanding of their nature. The poor citizen, the perhaps not very bright citizen, may not be able to *do* very much. But so far as he can *do* at all he has a claim, as good as that of the most proficient and active of his neighbors, to all the rights and opportunities which a democracy can provide.

These two points, that the citizen is an actor, a doer, who

is called by the traditions of the West to three distinct, though often contradictory, occupations, constitute a working definition of what it means to be a democratic citizen. And the first question to be asked is, what is the relationship between this citizen and the context in which he must live and work? For political philosophy, this question is put in the form of asking for the relationship between the citizen and his state because the state is not only the most important political fact in the citizen's environment. The state, particularly the modern state, may well be also the most important of all the facts in his environment.

The propensity of much of modern thinking on this question is to say that the relationship between the citizen and his state should be defined in terms of some one combination or another of rights *and* obligations. That is, the citizen receives rights and other privileges from the state, and it is only practical and fair, on a kind of *quid pro quo* basis, to insist that the citizen is obliged to use his rights and other opportunities in a responsible way. In more general terms, it is often said that there can be no freedom without responsibility. There is, of course, much truth in this conception. Within an actual social context, it is only realistic to recognize that none of us will long enjoy our individual rights unless we all allow to our neighbors much the same freedoms we claim for ourselves. We are also obliged to use our rights intelligently. Abuse of rights, even if only by neglect, will certainly cause trouble. But these observations are practical, however important, and are not profound. If taken without caution, they would seem to imply, first, that the principle for determining what rights a citizen should have is no more than "I'll scratch your back if you will scratch mine." What is to be done if a man discovers that he can arrange things so that he can obtain what he wants without any reciprocity on his part? Secondly, these observations seem to imply that if we abuse our rights we may be obliged to use them better. But if we are obligated to use our rights one way rather than another, can we fairly be said to have rights at all?

The Western tradition insists that the state cannot make a man good, that "compulsory morality is a contradiction in terms." From this it is argued that the state, if it is to be legitimate, must grant such rights to men as will allow them to make themselves good. If these rights are to be meaningfully possessed, their possession must be the guarantee that within certain areas citizens will be free to do exactly as they see fit. Political rights must bring, to use an old word, "license," even if only within sharply defined limits. In these areas, the citizen must be free to act, do, and pursue, governed only by his own conscience. Rights are meaningless if the state and public opinion hover about their exercise to ensure that they are used in the proper way, that they are not abused. Rights do not and should not be thought to imply political obligations. Within their limits they imply no political obligations at all. We may be dismayed at the way in which certain of our neighbors exercise their rights, but, politically and so long as they have their rights, there is nothing we or the state can do about it.

On the other hand, democratic citizens are, of course, obligated to use their rights in some ways rather than others, but this obligation is moral, not political, and it does not arise from any dictation by the state or from any responsibility assigned by the state. Morally, the citizen is obligated to use his rights only as means to the accomplishment of those three occupations to which his citizenship has committed him. There are requirements in all of those occupations which compel, although again the compulsion is moral, the citizen to allow to his neighbors many of the rights he expects for himself. He cannot participate unless he lives in a community of participation. He cannot serve unless others do too. His heritage will teach him, if nothing else will, that his private responsibility to seek out God comes to him only as it comes equally to all men.

But the democratic citizen is not only compelled, morally, to use his rights and to grant rights to his neighbors. He is compelled to regard the whole range of his state and his society as instruments by which and through which he may do and act as he must.

It is true that when the state, in its power, compels action, the only obligation present is that involved in either brute response to physical force or in the performance prompted by the unworthy motive of fear. And it is true also that the state must always be able to oblige performance in one or another of these senses. The practical sovereignty of any state must be absolute. The first duty of any state must be to keep the peace—to ensure, in other words, its own preservation. For this end, it holds for itself a monopoly of force ("murder"), and will strive by all means to eliminate any competitors arising in its jurisdiction. This is true whether or not a state is said to have a "limited" government, for all states must claim to be able to maintain peace, order, and defense within their own boundaries. As a result, it is the state and not the citizen which, practically, must be held responsible for the form and function of the system of law and public service which it maintains.

Yet it is also true that "will not force is the basis of the state." As a sociological fact, a state will not have power unless and until it is *em*powered by its citizens. In the West, no state can be legitimate unless it exists by the "consent" of its members; that is, the only legitimate state is one which understands itself to be, for all its sovereign power, the servant of the people. No one can deny that political obligation is obligation—and this in a purely coercive sense. But the West will refuse to regard the matter only in that light. Political obligation must in fact have, and will always in the West be insisted to have, a moral basis. In the West, the citizen, not the state, has the ultimate moral responsibility for what the state is. The citizen can and must regard the system of law and public service maintained by the state as being instruments for the use of himself and his fellows in their pursuit of the occupations of citizenship. The citizen is morally compelled to make use of his rights. He is under the same moral obligation to make comparable use of all his legal opportunities, of all the services provided by the state, even of the obedience which it exacts. In short, although it is sovereign, the citizen is obliged, morally, to use the state in all that it allows and in all that it compels.

What this means for any attempt to define citizenship in terms of its rights *and* obligations is that, in the first instance, citizenship is not a bundle of rights *and* obligations, but is rather a compound of obligations alone, these being, of course, all moral obligations. Because of his commitment to the occupations of citizenship, the citizen is morally obliged to obtain rights for himself and to use them intelligently. He is obliged to allow rights to his neighbors. He is obliged to accept services from the state and to demand them when necessary for himself and his neighbors. And he is obliged to obey the state, if it is a legitimate one, not only because he must in any case but also because he ought to. Only when this is clearly understood can we go on and admit that, within the actual political context and only as viewed from within that context, citizenship can be defined in law as being a combination of political rights and political obligations.

The relationship which these arguments postulate as existing between the state and the citizen is, then, a double one. From the point of view of the state, a practical view, the state is master and must be. The citizen receives from it certain rights and is compelled by it to perform certain obligations. But from the point of view of the citizen, a moral view, the state is servant, is an instrument by which the citizen can seek to do what he must. Not only that. The state must be for the citizen the primary agent for ordering the citizen's social context. It must be this because it alone has—and must have if the social peace is to be kept —the power. In so far as human ingenuity and resources permit change and control of our environment, the state is practically responsible for the condition of our society. If we are free and believe a diversity of views, that is because the state has allowed this situation to develop. If we have not all been "brain-washed" into believing one dogma, that is because the state has not chosen to "brain-wash" us. The only way to absolve the state of practical responsibility for the condition of our society is to show that the state, as a practical matter, is powerless to alter the situation.

As I suggested before, Americans generally cannot be expected to like this insistence that the citizen must give the state primary responsibility for ordering the social context. I do not particularly like it myself. But I can see no way to deny it. And beyond that, in this age when the potential practical power of the state is being enhanced on every side by the techniques of modern science, I think it is high time we recognized the state, even our democratic one, for what it is. Americans regularly protest that they have assigned to the state only a certain limited number of functions. But they seem quite blind to the fact that in granting the state the power to perform these functions they have granted it potentially absolute power. The limitations, constitutional and otherwise, with which we surround our state are meaningful only as they are interpreted and applied to the exercise of state power by the state itself. It is all the more important, therefore, to stress the citizen's moral responsibility for what the state is and does. The citizen must, to the limit of his abilities and within every opportunity the state allows, do all he can to ensure that the state's power is used wisely and for moral ends. Fortunately, our democratic state allows us many such opportunities. Fortunately, too, our state does much both to enable and to encourage us to make use of them.

All of this argument has been preparation for a more direct confrontation of the questions of what rights and obligations the citizen should expect from his state and of what place individualism may have among these. To the general question there can now be supplied the following general answer. The state must be expected to provide the citizen with that system of rights and obligations which will best enable him, with and among all his fellows, to participate in the civic life of his community, to serve loyally in the mission to which his nation has been called, and, in some measure, to go his own way in pursuit of his private destiny.

A number of observations must be made about this principle. The first is that the state, obviously, is going to have the greatest difficulty in performing the task thus assigned. The needs to be met, as we can never tire of saying, are both distinct and contradictory. But we still insist that the state attempt to meet all of them, and simultaneously. It is well known that the democratic state is expected to do all it can to allow and enable a wide degree of civic participation. It must grant all the necessary rights—the rights to vote, to associate, to stand for office, and so forth—and it must protect their exercise. It must also do all it can to enable the citizens to participate: it must maintain systems of public education; if necessary, it must discipline the press; it must tolerate within its own workings the not inconsiderable burden arising from the requirement that it be a public government operating in the fullest public view. And at the same time, the democratic government is expected to grant the citizen all those rights, and enforce all those obligations which will allow him to go his own way. Freedom of religion is only one example of this. Finally, the democratic state would certainly be held derelict, although the problem is rarely put in this form and with good reason, if it failed to maintain not only internal peace and order but also such armed forces and foreign missions as would permit the individual citizen to feel, whether he served directly or not, that he was a member of a community proudly sharing the full measure of its historic responsibilities. The use or nonuse, for example, of atomic weapons is a matter the decision of which rests, under our laws, with one man. Yet it is also a matter of national concern, and all citizens should feel whatever shame or pride, guilt or nerveless determination to do what we see to be right, may result.

The second major observation to be made about this basic principle describing what the citizen should expect of his state follows closely on the first. It is that the business of designing, defining, and supplying, of allowing and enforcing, any particular system of political rights and political obligations in an actual situation is going to be, *always*, a matter of practical judgment involving the *ad hoc* settlement of many "hard" questions. In this business there are few certainties other than that all is uncertain. Freedom of speech, as once defined, may not always enable and protect us. It may sometimes imperil us, just as, conversely, compulsory military service, instead of being a necessary, even noble, thing, was once thought both practically unnecessary and morally debilitating.

How obvious this is, and yet, how difficult for Americans, with their particular traditions and training, to accept! There are no inherent political obligations, no inherent political rights, only good ones and bad ones, useful ones and pernicious ones. In some circumstances possession of a right may be morally justifiable; in others it may not be. All that inheres in the citizen as a citizen are obligations, moral obligations to pursue his occupations (and even these will not arise unless the citizen accepts the generality of the Western tradition of citizenship). In their pursuit, he will sometimes want these rights, at other times those; he will sometimes expect to be obliged by the state to do these things, at other times other things. The uncertainty, the necessity for the constant exercise of practical judgment and intelligence, arises not only because situations constantly change. It also arises because the demands which have to be met are incapable of exact and final definition. The contradictions in the demands of citizenship are permanent. Sometimes the citizen can bring himself to accept the *status quo;* he will understand that, for the present, the requirements of his citizenship are being met in a manner consistent with the best that can be expected under the circumstances. At other times, he will not be content and will find himself under a moral compulsion to vote against the government, form a party, write a book—or even foment a revolution. For those who want only peace, good order, and stability, and hope to achieve these through absolute definition of certain clear and permanent principles of law, citizenship in the Western tradition is a dangerous business.

These conclusions—that, ultimately, the citizen is responsible for ensuring that the state, in an area of very awkward practical judgment, does all in its power to maintain a system of rights and obligations which will both allow and enable the individual to participate, serve, and go his own way—are of considerable theoretical importance. Any defense of individualism which would be broadly based must begin with them for, in essence, they insist that the value of a social system is finally to be measured in terms of the extent to which it enhances the personal worth of the individuals within it. And from these conclusions it is possible to go on to inquire about the nature and number of, on the one hand, the rights and, on the other, the obligations which should be included in a social and political system suitable to an individualistic democracy.

The question about the types of political obligation which the conscientious citizen should expect a democratic state to enforce is, in its theoretical aspects, straightforward. The practical questions, which political obligations, in conjunction with what rights are to be enforced in any given, actual situation, are of a very different order of difficulty and provide the substance of most political debate in all democracies. Into this difficult, even dangerous, area I do not propose to venture far and what I have to say is largely intended to clarify certain questions of theory.

In the first place, there is a very large class of political obligations the citizen should expect his state to enforce, which are obligations in the strict sense. Taxes must be paid and criminal acts forbidden. Obviously, there are very many acts of this type which must be done, or, as the case may be, not done, before the citizen could even hope to participate, serve, or have any degree of privacy. The urgent questions are concerned with the number and the kind of actions which the state should compel. What should the state do and what should it stop doing? Very nearly all that can be done by way of answering this is to remark again that wisdom and judgment are always necessary. The general principle which is gaining increasing acceptance for delimiting the state's compulsive actions hardly does more than underscore this point.

According to this principle, in the light of the moral commitments of the citizen, the state should compel all those actions which will work to increase the citizen's internal capacity and external opportunities to achieve his moral welfare. This is a positive view and for a long time it was necessary to emphasize that the state did have a positive function. However negative fear of the law might seem, the law did have in it the positive function of increasing moral capacity and moral opportunity. But, obviously, this principle by itself is not enough; it would imply, by itself, that Johnny should be kept in school, compulsorily, until the age of ninety because by then he would be very wise indeed. Conceivably, the state could so order our lives that we would spend all our days becoming morally capable and creating moral opportunities for ourselves without once performing a moral act. There are, in fact, states which give some evidence of expending great effort to build new societies which can only be "enjoyed" by generations to come. But in the West, today's citizens are as important as tomorrow's, and somewhere the state must stop compelling and allow the citizens to get on with such capacities and opportunities as they may possess.

This limit is set by adding to the above principle a second one which simply contradicts it. The state should *never* compel those actions which, by being compelled, will deny men the freedom to use such moral capacity as they have to grasp such moral opportunities as come their way. Payment of taxes must be compelled because, if they are not, they obviously will not often be paid, and the work of the state will have to cease; but if their payment is compelled, citizens are denied the opportunity to pay in sole recognition of their debt to society and without reference to any unworthy fear of punishment for nonpayment.

Let no one suppose, while suggesting these or similar principles for delimiting the areas in which the state should compel action, that he has presented much practical advice. For those who are unaware that the state has a positive moral function, the statement of these principles is undoubtedly salutary. Their statement would be equally salutary for those who are unaware, or insufficiently aware, that men must be capable as well as free to be moral. Certainly, it would be wise to impress these principles upon those who are ignorant of the fact that nowhere in this area—not even in the epithets "socialistic," "communistic," "fascist"—are there hard and fast, clear-cut principles for determining either what the state must do or what the state must not do. But beyond this, principles of the sort given above teach little and guide less. We must be guided not by principles relating to state action but by the ideals, the occupations, which the citizen should seek to achieve.

Much the same observations have to be offered about the remaining types of political obligation which the citizen can expect to be provided in a modern and socially advanced democracy. These constitute the so-called "welfare services," although we should be careful to interpret the phrase broadly enough to include in it all those services which a state may offer its citizens: not only aid to the indigent but also the provision of postal services, roads, and, as was pointed out earlier, armed forces, foreign missions, and so forth. These are not political obligations in the strict sense because only in a few instances, and then only on occasions such as military service today, are citizens compelled by the state to avail themselves of the opportunities which the services create. But they are obligations in the sense that the state undertakes to offer them because it is believed that only the state, as the comprehensive agent of compulsion in society, can provide them or provide them as efficiently as they are needed.

As before, the burning question is, How many and which of all these services should the state provide? Again as before, the theoretical answer is very nearly vacuous. The state should provide all those services which, on balance, will leave citizens both more capable and more free to go about their business of being citizens. The basic considerations are the same. Men must be both capable and free to be moral. The state can provide much, but in so doing it often nullifies possibilities for moral expression. The state must provide roads. About that there is no argument. But the business of having roads provided by the state involves a great deal of compulsion. Taxes must be paid, builders compelled to fulfill their contracts, drivers must be licensed, and all sorts of traffic regulations must be enforced before wide use of the roads can be enjoyed. Yet, on balance, we all agree that citizens, by having roads, are both more capable and more free than they would be without them.

Exactly the same kind of argument should apply to much warmer debates, such as that currently going on about whether the state should provide a compulsory national health program. Certainly, a great deal of compulsion would be necessary in any such scheme, and doctors particularly, long accustomed to a more lenient way of life, would find it painful to discover that many of the opportunities, formerly open to them, to apply the ethics of their medical oaths on their own volition, had simply disappeared. But the essence of this argument is still whether such a scheme would, on balance, leave the citizens, including the doctors, more healthy, more capable, *and* more free to go about the business of being good citizens. The principles of state action do determine that the question must be put in this form. But they certainly do not answer the question. The answer can only come from the exercise of judgment, a judgment which is informed, beyond the principles, by both great wisdom about present capacities and possibilities and by clear realization of the nature of the occupations which the citizen should be both fit and free to pursue.

The final remark to be made about the types of political obligations which a democracy should be expected to enforce or, through its powers of enforcement, provide, is concerned with a type which is not different in kind but is merely somewhat puzzling and also much neglected by philosophers and politicians alike. That type is the service of leadership which should in every democracy emanate from its government. Governments command great respect, and there is a ready audience for all their pronouncements. They have unexampled resources of information and advice. The leadership which any particular government provides its citizens is often regarded, therefore, as the hallmark of its integrity. To what extent does the government seek out and formulate the needs of its society? To what extent does it propose, publicly, viable alternative solutions to these needs? To what extent does it enable and encourage extensive and meaningful discussions of these solutions?

It is becoming increasingly apparent that in the conditions and circumstances of the modern, mass democracies, a government may well be justified in deliberately cultivating the existence, not only within its own ranks but in the rest of society as well, of a cultural elite of some sort, trained and willing to undertake and to lead that constant discussion of great issues which is the life blood of the democratic process. Otherwise, the discussion may all too easily flounder into demagoguery. But this raises in a nice form the question of the limits of state activity. It is not merely a matter of how much leadership, with the answer being that there must be enough leadership to ensure that the discussion is informed but not so much that the discussion becomes one-sided and thereby stops. This problem can also be put in the form of asking for the justification of the privileges granted the leading citizens and denied to the ordinary citizens.

This question can only be legitimately put from the point of view of the state, for it is essentially one of justifying those exceptional privileges and resources which the state must reserve for the more able citizens in order to allow them to develop and put to good use their superior talents. No one citizen can claim these privileges for his own use in his own behalf. He is bound to recognize that in so far as he is an actor, so also is the next man, even though the comparison of talents may be invidious. He is bound to recognize that just as he must participate, serve, and make peace with his God, so also is it important that his neighbor should do the same. His ability to do these things better is in itself no cause for special consideration. But the point of view of the state is significantly different. The democratic state in itself has no occupations; it has only those given to it by its citizen body. As given, its chief occupation is to create the social conditions within which all citizens, even the least of them, can do what they must. Therefore, if the state, by granting privileges and creating an elite, can promote conditions in which all citizens, even the least, can better pursue their ideals, then it will be justified in doing so. Therefore also, the state may be justified in reserving for rank not only privileges but resources as well, if, by such reservation, all citizens become, on balance, more capable and freer than they were. The leading citizen can lay claim to his privileges only so long as he can persuade the state that his possession of them will continue in fact to contribute to this end.

The system of political rights and political obligations which a state maintains for the benefit of its citizens is a single system. It may have to help the citizens serve three occupations and bear the marks of the tensions between these but it is still one system and should be designed as such. All additions and emendations should be made with this fact in mind. There is little point in granting a man freedom of speech if his neighbors are not allowed to assemble to hear what he may wish to say. And there will be equally little point in allowing the neighbors to assemble if their meeting is not protected by the police from outside interference. Indeed, the police may have to be present at the meeting itself to ensure that it is conducted in the orderly way necessary to the meaningful exercise of free speech by individuals. No one right or obligation can be significant by itself. There must be a system of rights and obligations, each right and obligation of which presupposes the rest and works with the rest to secure to individuals the desired capacities and opportunities.

As a consequence, all the general considerations deduced above as applicable to political obligations will be equally applicable to political rights. I can therefore assume that, in so far as the reader has accepted the preceding argument, he will be willing to accept, without further argument, that the state should grant all those rights which will, on balance and always in conjunction with such political obligations as are also in force, leave the citizens more capable and more free to participate, serve, and go their own way. I assume that he will also accept that, in the question of which rights a citizen ought to have, there are no hard and fast, clear-cut principles and that great reliance must be placed on the exercise of judgment which takes into consideration the capacities of the citizens, their current circumstances, and a clear realization of the natures of the conflicting occupations which, in the West, good citizens must pursue. Very little more will be said here directly on the question of how to determine the rights which a democratic citizen should have.

But there are questions about rights which urgently require painstaking analysis. What are rights? What does it mean to possess them? How are they obtained and what form must their justification take? Some of these questions are rarely, if ever asked, particularly in America. The confusion which surrounds the nature of rights in this country is only partly caused by the fact that this is a subject which appears simple but is in reality very complex. It is also caused by the fact that in this country the philosophy in terms of which much of our discussion of rights is carried on, the doctrine of Natural Rights, falsely implies, as I have already suggested, both that the problem really is simple and that rights somehow inhere immediately in men as men. This situation should not go unchallenged. I have my own bias in favor of privacy, an area of freedom only to be secured by rights, but discussion of this subject is also demanded on the broader grounds that rights are not only essential to the democratic way of life but are also in many ways the most characteristic feature of political democracy.

I said that this analysis would be painstaking, and I begin with what may appear to be trivia. The word "right" can be used in several ways: "I am right in saying this," "I have a right to expect payment," and "I have the right to free speech." It is obvious that these three uses are distinct: the first implies only that "I" am correct or am justified; the second insists that "I" have a justifiable claim against someone; and the third proclaims that "I" am in possession of a certain freedom. It is just as clear that all these meanings are related, that, in fact, the third includes that of the other two as well as adding something of its own. For the full meaning of the third may be given as, "I am justified in saying that I have a claim to a certain freedom," or, more simply, "I have a justifiable claim to this freedom."

Most discussions of rights are in terms of the second of these meanings, the third being treated only as a special instance of it. Rights, that is, are defined only as justifiable claims and the notion that a right is a justifiable claim to a certain *freedom* is introduced only by way of illustration or for purposes of appended argument. This is a perfectly logical way of handling the matter. However, the special case of claims to freedom seems so important and raises so many questions of its own that I have conducted the whole of the following analysis in terms of it alone. Even so, many of the conclusions arrived at can be applied equally well to the more general character of rights where they are seen to be simply claims to receive certain goods and services, such as jury trial, payment of debts, police protection of the home, and so forth. For our purposes here, then, use of the word "right" implies claim, justification, *and* freedom. From this, much follows.

We must look more closely at the nature of the freedom to which claim is made by right. Reflection shows that the statement "I have the right to speak" does not proclaim "I *will* speak." The "I" may only be *reserving* the right for future use. What this suggests is that a claim to a right can be translated to mean, "I, and I alone, will decide what will be done, when and how, that within the limits of the right I, and I alone, am sovereign."

Three conclusions of primary importance to a theory of rights follow from this. First, rights, obviously, are freedoms. It is true, as was remarked before and will be again, that a right is a grant of freedom held in trust. But the moral obligation thus implied to use the right only for securing certain ends must not be allowed to obscure the fact that the possession of a right signifies the official absence of any kind of official compulsion to employ the right in one way rather than another.

Secondly, rights can only be possessed by "individuals," though the "individuals" may on occasion be collective bodies such as corporations, clubs, and the like. But whether single or collective, in order to exercise their rights they must act individually. Sovereignty is a logical concept and as such it is true by definition that in any one area two sovereigns are fully one too many.

Finally, it may be concluded from the above that the only individuals capable of possessing rights are those capable of making the decisions required for their exercise. Though we may have obligations of one sort or another to treat dogs in certain ways, it cannot be said that dogs have rights simply because we do not conceive of dogs being capable of deciding to act. It is probably from this feature, which insists that rights can only be possessed by individuals capable of "deciding to do," that rights derive their great appeal for citizens in the Western democratic tradition. In that tradition citizens are doers but always in a moral sense. They desire, therefore, not only the liberty which allows them to perform but also, and beyond that, the liberty which only rights can bring, the liberty of deciding for themselves if, when, and how they will perform their occupations. Only then can they hold themselves, and be held by others to be, morally responsible for their acts and their achievements.

The claim, then, which a right advances initially takes the form of "I and I alone will decide this matter." If this is allowed, then it must also be allowed that all this statement amounts to is an insistence that "*You* will *not* decide this matter." Again the argument appears almost too simple, but it establishes beyond rebuttal that if the claim to a right is to be meaningful, then there must be a social context within which the claim is advanced. This is even more obvious when it is realized that a right denies not only you the opportunity to decide for me, but denies that privilege to everyone. "I, alone" means, if anything, "No one save me."

This point reveals one of the primary functions of rights. Aristotle perceived long ago that some things in every society must be shared. Rights have the function of marking off some things which are *not* to be shared. If I have the right to free speech, I do not need to share with any the decisions about what I say. No wonder the citizen, anxious about his privacy, is concerned to look to the condition of his rights. Much of modern society, the things it does and the things it has, must be shared by all with all, but, in terms of our traditions, it will be a sorry day when everything must be. For in our tradition the citizen is both a part of a unit, society, and a unit himself; he is both social and autonomous. A primary function of rights is to ensure that the citizen is enabled to keep himself distinct from that of which he is also a part.

We must next look at the vexed process by which challenged claims to rights are justified. We must bear in mind here that, as a justifiable claim is not a challenge to a fight, so also it is not a command expecting obedience. If the claim, as justifiable, is to play a determining role in the dispute of which it is part, then the parties to that dispute must, for these purposes at least, be regarded as equals. If they are not so regarded, then, on the one side, there would be little point in examining the claim and, on the other, little hope or reason for advancing it. The claim must, therefore, add to the dispute some authority other than that which may be possessed by either party. Inasmuch as it is only the party against whom the claim is made who is to be bound, then this authority must be one which that party, at least, but not necessarily also the claimant, recognizes as having jurisdiction both over him and in the matter in dispute.

The number of types of authority, men being such as they are, which might thus be recognized as appropriate is legion. Depending only on the subject of the dispute and the beliefs of the parties concerned, the authority may be God, or a book, or a set of ethics, or a state, or an official of some sort, or merely some end the achievement of which is desired. In this last example, the claim to a right might be phrased, "I wish this right and I know that you wish to achieve that end. Do you not see that in order to achieve your end, you must allow me the freedom I desire?"

This analysis puts us in a position to state consecutively all the steps in the process by which rights are claimed and justified and finally granted. A name, even, can be given to this process which will give all these steps some symmetry, "The Triangularity of Rights." But before these steps are listed, the simplest of examples of disputed rights may provide perspective.

Johnny is discovered at the cookie jar by elder sister Janie. Janie says, "You can't do that!" Johnny replies, "Yes I can! Mommy said I could." Notice that Johnny does not say "Mommy told me to." He is laying claim to a right by possession of which he is entitled to decide for himself whether, when, and how many cookies he will eat. And the emphatic character of his claim suggests that, beyond Janie's going off to "check" with Mommy, the matter will rest here. It might not, however, if Johnny had said, "Yes I can. Aunt Alice said I could." Janie might not recognize Aunt Alice as an authority, or, if she did, not as an authority for her, or, failing that, not an authority recognized by her as empowered to decide questions involving Johnny and cookies.

All the following steps are involved both in this example, however implicitly, and, it is suggested, in any situation concerning disputed rights. An "I" presents, against a "you," a claim that a certain right be allowed (step 1). When this is queried, the "I" cites authority (step 2) and receives from it the permission, or particular sovereignty, which is the substance of the right (step 3). The "you" then consults the authority, recognizes it as one for him and appropriate to the matter at hand (step 4), and receives from it notification that the right has been duly granted to the "I" (step 5). Finally, the "you" allows the "I" his right and, for the first time, it can be said to be actually possessed (step 6).

This analysis of the steps in the process by which claims to rights are justified establishes a conclusion, about the nature of the social context within which rights must appear, which can be put in a number of ways. In the first place, this analysis warrants an insistence that not only must rights appear only in a social context but also that this context must be one of a society in which there are recognized patterns and relationships for establishing and maintaining social discipline. There is an element of command between the authority and the "you." This must be firm and must imply that if the "you" does not allow the right, sanctions of some sort will be forthcoming. This point can also be put by saying that a right, to be possessed, must have been granted and that an unrecognized right is not a right possessed. This is a more usual way of putting the matter and it is particularly relevant for those philosophers, such as Locke and the authors of the Declaration of Independence, who seemed to think that rights could be discussed in a social vacuum. Finally, the matter can be expressed by saying that there is a great difference between asking "Do I have this right?" and asking "Ought I to have this right?" This distinction supplies the answer to those who complain that they have been injured despite what *they* think are their rights. To desire a right is only the first step in the long series necessary to its ultimate receipt.

This raises the question of how to get a right we desire but, in fact, do not possess. How do we go about persuading the relevant authorities to make the grant in terms of which our neighbors may be compelled to allow us the right we desire? A distinction must be made here between the process the argument must go through and the grounds from which it is legitimate to advance the argument.

Most of our disputes about rights are with our neighbors and for the settlement of these we turn ultimately to the state, that agent in society which claims to be the final arbitrator of all our quarrels. Suppose that we have engaged in such a quarrel and that, upon being taken to the state, the case is settled against us. The matter need not rest here, for in every society there is a hierarchy of authorities. Our neighbors are, for the moment, content, for the settlement of the case has shown that the state does not grant and will not enforce the right we wish them to allow us. But we can turn upon the state to begin a new argument in which we will seek to show that the state must allow us the right because it has been granted to us by the authority under which the state operates, namely, the opinions of society generally. The state may prove unimpressed by the opinions of society (in which case we may resort to "revolution" though perhaps only to the extent of willfully breaking the state's law and serving our sentence in order to signalize to society the state's truculence toward its views), or we may discover that the state is justified in believing that society has not made any such grant of a right to us. But again we can begin a further dispute, this time with society, and the authority now would be the traditions and accepted ethics of the society. We may lose even this argument on the basis that there is nothing in those traditions and ethics to compel social opinion to grant the right we desire (in which case we would have to convert society to a new ethic, a long process). But if we triumph and the grant is shown to have been made, we can go back to the state with our new warrant, demand from it an endorsement, and return to present a complete claim on our neighbors.

This is the process which we must follow if we are to force recognition of a right we do not have but which we desire. Something remains to be said about the character of the actual argument to be used by a claimant to a right in presenting his case to the relevant authority. The first thing to be noticed is the character of rights as means to the achievement of ends. We do not wish to have freedom of speech unless we have some intention of speaking, if not immediately at least one day when we have something to say. It is sometimes said that we ought to love freedom for itself. There may be persons who do love freedom in this way, but if they do it is because they want freedom in order to achieve the end of feeling free—although more probably they wish freedom to achieve ends to which, at the moment, they are unable to give articulate definition.

More to the point, citizens in the Western tradition do have ends they wish to achieve, the performance of their three occupations. They will demand rights because the liberty which the possession of rights provides will enable them to work toward these ends as, within the limits of the rights, they see fit. Their argument for a right as yet ungranted will simply be that it is required by them if their purposes are to be accomplished. This, by itself, is not, however, enough to persuade the relevant authorities. Those authorities must be persuaded and by argument alone. If the claimant could somehow force the grant of a right by the authorities without argument he would hardly need to have it granted to him, nor would he have much need to insist that others be compelled by the authorities to allow him to exercise it freely. Thus the claimant, even though he is not necessarily required to recognize the authority as one for him, must still, in a sense, beseech the authority to grant him the right. He can only do this if he can establish, in addition to the fact that possession of the right by him will achieve a certain end, two further points. First, he must establish that the end to be achieved is good, and good not only in his own eyes but in those of the authority as well. Secondly, he must prove that it is he who should achieve it.

This last requirement is crucial. It may be fairly easy to demonstrate to an authority that the end to be achieved by possession of a right is worth while, and is an end which the authority, for some one reason or another, would like to see achieved. But it may be much more difficult to persuade the authority that it ought to be achieved by the claimant rather than by some other, perhaps more skillful, individual. When a social ethic is the relevant authority, it may speak in blunt terms: All men, regardless of their individual talents, should have the rights necessary to achievement of these ends. But when the relevant authority is the state itself, harried and weighed down by the burdens of daily government in the modern age, we may be hard put to argue persuasively that, for example, all citizens, not excepting the stupid, the ignorant, and, yea, even the wicked, should have a voice and a vote in framing the great policies of the nation.

It is because these requirements are so stringent—that the argument for the grant of a right must show the end which possession of the right is designed to achieve, must show that this end is good, and must show that it is good to have the claimant achieve it—that some have jumped to the conclusion that rights cannot be had unless they are granted reciprocally by all to all. If this is true, then it becomes exceptionally easy to show that I must grant the rights I want for myself to everybody else because only then can I expect everybody else to grant those rights to me. But we know that this is not true. As we have shown earlier, no necessity for reciprocity is contained in the process by which claims to rights are justified. I do not claim my rights on the grounds that I have given something to somebody else. I claim my rights because I need them, because they are necessary to my accomplishment of certain ends.

It may have been in part the knowledge of this defect that has prompted the more sophisticated version of this same thesis. This version, on the basis that rights are only meaningful as parts of a social system, insists that I only receive my rights as I become a member of a social system, as I become a member of an actual society. It then says that, in becoming a member of a society and thereby receiving my rights from it, I, to that extent, pledge myself to accept as a good for me the common good of the society and therefore also, to the same extent, pledge myself to use my newly received rights only for the general welfare of the community of which I am now a member.

The conclusion that is drawn from all this, besides the formal one that there can be no recognition of rights without there also being a recognition of a common good, is that it will be to the interest of all to grant me my rights because I will use them to work with all for a good common to all and that it will equally be to my interest, and for the same reasons, to grant the appropriate rights to all other members of the community and to all officers of its state.

This version of what might be called the reciprocity thesis deserves a good deal of respect. It is true that rights are only to be had within a social context. It is true also that in any society there must be a very general amount of agreement about the ends which the rights granted by society are supposed to achieve. No society will long survive if the ends which its various citizens seek to achieve are widely divergent. Even more, it is true that in any healthy society there must be, as this version of the reciprocity thesis correctly implies, a very large measure of trust, of willingness to believe that nearly everybody *will* use his rights in ways which will be to the betterment of society or at least not actively injurious to its welfare. No state would be justified in granting rights except in the hope—which would have to be a great deal more than merely pious— that the great generality of citizens will not "abuse" them.

But this version of the reciprocity thesis can be fairly charged with having "jumped" to its conclusions. It has failed to note that in moving from a discussion of the nature of rights to considerations about the necessity of wide measures of agreement and trust in any society, it has drastically shifted its grounds of argument. The nature of rights can be arrived at by simple, even if lengthy, analysis. The requirements of a healthy society, however, can only be discovered by practical observation and the conclusions thus arrived at are of a different order from those arrived at by analysis of the logical implications and involvements of a concept. This error might be allowed to pass except for the fact that it has prompted the conclusion that rights can *only* be had when there is mutual recognition by all of a common good on behalf of which all will exercise their rights. This conclusion the traditions of Western citizenship will not tolerate.

Again, it is admitted that there are obvious requirements for any healthy society and certainly a great many rights will have to be consistently used for the accomplishment of what we may call public purposes. But the requirement that before a right can be granted it must be shown that the end it will help achieve is good does not necessarily insist that this end can only be good as it is good *for* society (or other relevant authority). Rights are social and the ends for which they are designed must be acknowledged by society as good. But the members of the society may well grant me my rights simply because they feel some moral compulsion to do so. They may well feel that unless I am allowed to pursue freely certain ends they will not be able to justify themselves in terms of their own traditions. Some of the traditions of the West, as I have insisted, are exactly of this character.

The third strand of our traditional citizenship insists that we are all members of a great community and that as members of that community we are all obligated to respect and honor each other. Chief among these obligations is that we should grant to each other such rights and privileges as are necessary to allow each citizen the opportunity to pursue his private occupation. The goods to be achieved in that occupation and by the rights which allow its performance are goods in the eyes of the community but they are private goods. They are private goods because the occupation which each pursues is a private one. Society may, in fact, have to pay a considerable price to allow their achievement but, in the West, that price must, in measure, be paid. There must be a recognition of a common good, in some sense, in any society, but this does not preclude either the recognition of private goods as good or the granting of rights for their achievement.

The conclusions to which this analysis of the nature of rights has arrived, as well as something of the character of the rights which a democracy ought to grant its citizens, can be summarized if an attempt is made to provide a system of nomenclature for rights. A usual division is between public and private rights. But before any such titles can be used, it must be recognized that *all* rights contain within them both a public element and a private element. The public element derives from the fact that any meaningful right can only be possessed when it has been granted by a public authority within a social context. The private element derives from the fact that a right thus possessed assigns to some individual the opportunity or permission to make decisions by himself and for himself. If we consistently recognize these essential features of rights, we can go on to classify them.

One way to do this would be by reference to the authority which grants the rights. On this basis, political rights would be those granted by the state and enforced by its courts and police. Social rights would be those granted by social opinion and "enforced" by the same. Moral rights would be those granted by an accepted ethic and "enforced" by the feelings of guilt engendered in those who, while accepting it, did not obey its maxims. A more usual and perhaps also more useful basis of classification is by reference to the kind of ends which the rights are designed to achieve. Here the categories are very numerous, for we can have political rights, business rights, private rights, public rights, family rights, rights of association and so on indefinitely.

Finally, rights can be classified by reference to the community which, together, the "I," the "you," and the relevant authority, make up. Thus we can have national rights and church rights, family rights, local rights, professional rights, and so forth. The very variety of possible classifications serves to underline the complexity of this matter and emphasizes the fact that the full story about any one right cannot be known until it is told who grants the right, to whom, the end which possession of it is supposed to achieve, together with a list of the persons commanded to allow it.

The conclusions to which this chapter has brought us thus far may be summarized as follows. First, no defense of democracy, or of the individualism essential to it, can begin except by establishing the notion that the citizen is an actor, a doer but is one who must always act and do within the confines of his society.Therefore, the citizen must look to the state, the prime and final instrument for the ordering of the social context, for the establishment of the basic framework within which citizens may pursue their three occupations. From this, and other considerations, it follows that the citizen, despite the practical sovereignty of the state, is morally responsible for ensuring that the state does provide a framework of rights and obligations suitable to democratic individualism.

Secondly, the social and legal framework, which the conscientious citizen must demand that his state provide, is a single system, although composed of numerous political obligations, on the one hand, and, on the other, political rights. The task of designing and supplying such a system is an extraordinarily difficult one. It is difficult because the three occupations, all of which the system must allow and enable the citizen to undertake, are so contradictory. And it is also difficult because the situations, within which the system must exist and within which the occupations are to be performed, are constantly changing. The long and pains-taking analysis we have given of the nature of political obligations and of political rights establishes this beyond doubt. Political rights and obligations are means, no more, and the questions about the number and type of each which must be supplied by the state can only be answered by the exercise of a widely informed practical judgment. Much information must be had about actual conditions. Even more important, there must be a clear understanding of the ends which rights and obligations are to achieve, of the occupations which the heritage of the West calls on democratic citizens to perform.

This reiteration of the need for wisdom and the exercise of an informed practical judgment is depressing. It is de-pressing whether the need is stated bluntly or arrived at again as a conclusion to a long and painstaking analysis of the institutions, political rights and political obligations, through which the ideals of our citizenship have to be achieved. It is all the more depressing when we recall the need for a firm and forthright defense of that critical, third aspect of our citizenship, individualism. To devise a system of rights and obligations by which citizens would be allowed and enabled to pursue the ends of the first two aspects of their citizenship, participation and service, ap-pears to be a relatively easy matter. Certainly there would

be complications, but the patterns of democratic participation are well known, and the calls of history upon our
nation and its citizens are, if anything, too imperative and
too insistent.

But to devise in the modern environment a system of
rights and obligations, or, rather, to include in one system
the further rights and obligations necessary for the pursuit of the third occupation besides those necessary for the
other two, must be a very difficult business. This must be
especially the case now when, not only is society in its many
manifestations closing in upon us all, but so also are its
values, values which, by our heritage, we share with it. Yet,
because of this necessity for great wisdom and judgment,
there is very little that can be done to help devise such a
system of rights and obligations by persons not actively
engaged in the attempt to keep an actual system of this
sort operating in a particular environment. With reference
to the weakened condition of individualism, the most that
the philosopher can do is to state more fully than we yet
have the vital importance of this third strand of our citizenship to the whole of the democratic way of life and to examine some of the requirements which will have to be met
if it is to be a vigorous influence in our society.

If it is allowed that the rights which give citizens freedoms are a first characteristic of political democracy, then
it must also be allowed that the philosophy of individualism, as we have inherited the pattern of it in the West, is
a first characteristic of the democratic way of life. The
pattern of this individualism, as we have argued before, is
the source of the democratic view of the equality of man.
The insistence that all men are actors, are sources of
energy, together with the view that, as an actor, each man
is entitled to a private occupation and to a citizenship in a

community which transcends that of particular place, compels the admission that each man in any particular society must be treated as a man.

This same insistence is also the source of the democratic justification of toleration. The argument is often put that few men are really tolerant or can afford to be. With the generality of men what happens is that all the strife and pain which are the price of attempts to enforce intolerance periodically lull men into an indifference toward each other's beliefs. It is to this indifference that they then apply the high-sounding title of "The Spirit of Toleration." Plausible as this is, it amounts to no more than an explanation of why many men are, in fact, sometimes tolerant and it provides no grounds whatever for justifying why we should be tolerant whether we wish to be or not.

That justification, in the Western tradition of citizenship, stems from the insistence that every man must be recognized as a citizen and, as such, is morally entitled to find his own way and seek out his own truth. On this view, it makes no difference whether he is this or that or some other cog in the social machine of this society. He is always also a citizen of another community and as in that community he is not only entitled but morally compelled to discover such beliefs for himself as he can.

Besides being the source of these general beliefs characteristic of democracy, the presence of individualism in our citizenship also transforms the character of the other two occupations into something quite different from what they otherwise would be. When the individualistic citizen participates in the civic life of his community, he will bring to it a far greater sense of his own individuality and of the distinctiveness of his own personality than was ever characteristic of the Athenian citizen. This, at least potentially, will add greatly to the vitality of the civic life. The individualistic citizen, in so far as he really is individualistic, will be far less susceptible than the Athenian to mass appeals, far more insistent that political argument address itself directly to his own understanding.

More important, the old atmosphere of exclusiveness, to the extent to which the ideals of individualism are in fact accepted, will have to go. The citizenship will have to be a broad one and also an open one. It is the influence of these tendencies toward individualistic participation and broad citizenship which has created the modern ideal of the democratic process as one in which all the devices of government, elections, congresses, public government, and so forth, are seen primarily as means for ensuring that as many as possible contribute, significantly, to the discussion of the great issues confronting the state.

Finally, the philosophy of individualism has demanded a very considerable narrowing of the Greek view of the dimensions of politics. The state, the individualist insists, is primarily to be identified by its possession of its power to *compel* obedience. As such its morally deadening influence must be withdrawn from every possible area in which citizens can be safely left to find their own way without causing serious injury to either themselves or the state.

The impact of individualism on the notion of the loyal citizen has been equally decisive. To a large extent, individualism has determined the content of the mission which the democratic nation and its citizens must serve. Under its influence, that mission has been to establish here a democratic way of life in which individualism has its due place, to preserve that way of life, and to urge its extension to other areas of the world.

At the same time, the influence of individualism has drastically curbed the techniques available to democracy for accomplishing its mission and has set limits on the degree of service which it can legitimately demand from its own citizens. The techniques must be those which, because of the values cherished by individualism, rely ultimately not on coercion for conversion to democratic beliefs but rather on rational argument. In fact, they must rely on an argument which hardly does more than point, though again and again, to the values which democrats cherish. The same reasoning places limits on the amount of service to be expected from citizens. A democracy must constantly bear in mind that, by its own creed, the commitment of its citizens to it cannot be total, that the citizens have other things to do which have a moral legitimacy as great as any of its own projects.

Finally, the individualistic citizen brings to his loyal service to the state the sense of personal responsibility for his own acts. He of course brings this also to his participation in the democracy's civic life, but the sense of personal responsibility is obviously of more critical value when the question is of the citizen's loyalty. The state, in demanding service, expects performance. But it must, particularly in modern conditions, predict performance and predict also absence of deliberate subversion. Democracies are fortunate that the trust which they must put in their citizens can be supported by appeals to the sense of personal and moral responsibility of each man for his own acts.

More generally and of far greater significance, it is from the philosophy of individualism that democracy ultimately gains its claims to legitimacy. Judged on the basis of its ability to achieve the ends described in the citizen's first two occupations—particularly the second, the mission in history—judged, in short, "pragmatically"—democracy is sometimes cantankerous, as often frenzied, and much of the time merely lethargic. It is always cumbersome and its operation is always plagued by the ignorance and petty vices of the many—that is, by the sins of us all. In no system of government are stupidities and evils given such opportunity for constant, harassing, and cumulative effect. If there are truly barbaric impulses at large in society, democracy often seems unable to tame them. In any case, critics are regularly provided at least plausible grounds for arguing that this or that democracy is on the road to ruin.

But the claim of the democratic society is that, if it be on such a road, at least it will arrive at its destination legitimately. Democracies do not need to insist—and are certainly both unwise and morally wrong if they do—that because they are democracies, they will be more successful, more triumphant than other types of government. But they must claim that what they do they try to do in ways that are morally defensible. And this claim stems ultimately from the strain of individualism in democratic citizenship. In a democracy, the state, for all its leadership, for all its necessary powers of compulsion, is yet the servant of society, is yet no more than an instrument by which citizens seek their appointed ends. The moral values implicit in the philosophy of individualism insist that the state never aspire to more than this. These values insist that the state strive no more than to enable its citizens to pursue and pursue freely their three occupations, whatever the contradictions between those occupations and whatever difficulties lie in the way of their accomplishment.

It is this characteristic of democracy, stemming from the individualism which, among other things, is inherent in it, which transforms the definition of democracy from a supposed objective description of a certain sort of state and society and their institutions, into a personal testament of how life in a society should be lived and how it should be understood. In the last analysis, democracy is not a basis for judging a government's performance in achieving the usual ends of such instruments. In the last analysis, democracy is a faith to be held by citizens about themselves, their society, and, only then, their state.

This is a measure of our need, as democrats, of a philosophy of individualism in the traditional pattern. What does it require of us? What sort of beliefs must we hold if this philosophy is to have a decisive influence in our society? The pattern of traditional individualism, as its genetic formation was outlined in an earlier chapter, has two major aspects, a notion of dual citizenship and a theory of private occupation. Both these aspects are in the tradition and both are necessary to it and to our belief in it.

The notion of dual citizenship is important because it provides the individual with a "first" citizenship which transcends that of any particular society. This serves to mark off and delimit the citizenship of any particular place and, as I have previously argued at length, such marking off and delimiting are useful advantages in themselves. But the transcendent citizenship has further advantages. By possessing it, the citizen of this or that community has, as we sometimes say, "a leg out." He has a ground of no little moral distinction from which to face his present society, to judge it, to criticize it both in itself and in its treatment of him.

Criticism of a society only on grounds and in terms of values and philosophies which that society provides for itself is usually petty, however searching the techniques. It can never be substantial or challenging of the very vitals of that society's existence. But the criticism by the democrat, because of his, in a sense, "external" citizenship, can always potentially be searching in both technique and substance. Moreover, all the citizens share this transcendent citizenship. They can therefore converse with each other in terms over which their present societies have no sovereignty. They can share their criticisms, compare them, and agree on what changes they should demand of their present communities. Finally, the transcendent citizenship gives to each individual a substance, a reality, a significance quite apart from that which comes to him by his membership in an actual community. He is important and not only because he fulfills adequately this or that role in the present society.

But what sort of vision of a greater community is possible for Americans today? It is doubtful if it would be either possible or even desirable to attempt to resuscitate the kind of vision which Jefferson and Tom Paine possessed, with its great dependence on a rationalistic universe and a rigid interpretation of the nature of Natural Law. When that vision went, it took with it a lot of other beliefs, some of which we might not be too eager to see return.

The Christian vision of a Brotherhood of Man under the kingship of the Christian God is a more hopeful one. Christianity is a living faith and widely dispersed. It contributed far more directly to the basic values of democracy than did the rather arid doctrines of the Enlightenment. Further, the doctrinal and sectarian differences, particularly in the United States, have so softened the outlines of this vision of the Brotherhood of Man, both in respect to the nature of the community and to the nature of the God who rules it and supplies it with its law, that it has become something which can be shared easily by Christians in their multitudinous diversity and also by Jews and by many nonformally religious persons. On the other hand, it yet retains a definable character. However broad its range of tolerance, the modern notion of the Brotherhood of Man still insists upon firm agreement about certain basic values and attitudes concerning the obligations which men owe to each other and to themselves.

The task, then, would be to point anew to this aspect of Christian doctrine, to re-emphasize it, to give it, perhaps, more immediate meaningfulness by insisting that not only are all Christians members of the brotherhood but so also are all Americans and all the citizens of America's democratic allies. Obviously, there are many peoples of the world who do not belong to this brotherhood. (This, incidentally, precludes the notion of "humanity" being a satisfactory transcendent community for democrats.) They do not share our basic values and would deny us our present opportunities of allegiance to them if they dared or could. But many peoples do belong to it and they include far more than just Americans. But whether the Brotherhood of Man can be or will be thus revived and reunderstood is a matter about which I do not presume to say anything here.

The traditional philosophy of individualism has a need for a theory of private occupation which is equally demonstrable. It is, in fact, much more obvious and readily admitted. A theory of private occupation gives to the vision of the transcendent community a substance and vitality, a meaningfulness and purpose which it would not otherwise have, and in so doing it brings these same virtues to the philosophy of individualism as a whole. Even more obviously, a private occupation gives to each member of the transcendent community, and to each of us in the course of our ordinary lives, something to do, a task to occupy and to justify our possession of privacy. Without it, our possession and our claims to be allowed privacy would become pointless.

So again we must ask the question, what kind of private occupation is possible for Americans today? Here there are certain obvious requirements. It must, in the first place, be an occupation which can qualify as being genuinely private, that is, it must be one in which the goods achieved in it can be reasonably viewed as accruing primarily to the persons performing it. On the other hand, the public consequences resulting inevitably from any human activity, no matter how passive, must not impose an intolerable strain on the community and its projects. It would be tolerable to define the private occupation in such a way as to require neighbor to knock on my door and enter only when admitted. It would not be tolerable to define the private occupation in terms of having me supply neighbor with his dinner, particularly if I frequently decided not to supply it. On this basis, it is clear that the definition given by many nineteenth-century industrialists of private, free enterprise capitalism as a private occupation is an aberration of what is required by the traditional philosophy of individualism. At the other extreme, it is equally clear that to define the occupation as being the devotion of all our efforts to being public citizens and doing good in society is again an aberration of the tradition. Such definition fails both on the count that such a citizen's multifarious activities would have to be submitted to many controls imposed by the state, and that he would have to submit much of what he thinks is "doing good in society" to the approval of his fellow citizens, but it fails also on the count that the good which would accrue to him would only be an incidental by-product of all such good as he might accomplish.

These requirements suggest that the appropriate private occupation will have to be something close, if not to that which Augustine finally defined for himself, then at any rate close to that process, that quest for wisdom, which he pursued before eventually arriving at his own definition. Such a definition was for a long time strongly present in the American tradition and is the source of much of our philosophy of public education. It has influenced us strongly toward mass education. Moreover, it has influenced us strongly into believing that all, even the stupid, should be trained in the liberal, and not just the civic, arts, regardless of practical vocation.

This tradition in our immediate heritage can be revived. We can come to say again that each man, each citizen no matter who, should be enabled and encouraged to learn for himself such truth as he can find. We can come to say again that he must reach this truth for himself, that he must be capable and free to form such opinions as he will about the nature and meaning of his own existence. Some, of course, will say that this is not always important. We must have a roof over our heads even before we can sit down to eat. Some will say that it matters not a whit to the quality of the shoes if the cobbler understands, or is trying to learn, what his own opinions are about his place in history and the universe. But these persons are not democrats. The cobbler is more than a cobbler. In the democratic society, he is also always a man, a citizen, and this stature he carries with him when he participates in the civic life of his community, serves in its historic mission, goes his own way—or simply sits and cobbles.

We cannot say whether this, or the other, aspect of traditional individualism will be revived. But we can say that rights which can enable us to live that philosophy are granted by society, and that, therefore, there must be a general social acceptance of these beliefs before you and I can expect to have such rights and exercise them freely. We are not entitled to say whether American society will, or even, with precision, the extent to which it must, recapture the spirit of individualism. But we can, with some safety, predict that unless America has this spirit, democracy here will change in both content and form—and will change radically.

In sum, individualism cannot be revived and defended anew in America unless the commitment to it in the traditional form is renewed. There is no question that we have been individualists and that our democracy has been shaped in the past to meet our requirements as individualists. But whether this will continue to be the case can only be settled by the people themselves. Either Americans will be individualists and cherish the values of individualism or they will not. If they are true to their traditional heritage, then their democracy as traditionally formed can be defended. If they choose to abandon their heritage there is little that philosophers, as philosophers, can do. Individualism requires certain institutions, most notably the kind of rights which democracies have usually supplied, in order to fulfill itself. Those institutions can be defended on the basis that they meet the requirements of individualism as traditionally understood. The rights proclaimed in the Declaration of Independence and spelled out in the Bill of Rights can be defended on the basis that they serve the values inherent in individualism of the traditional sort. They certainly cannot be defended by any assertion that somehow we do, inalienably, already have them. But the individualism itself, that upon which all other argument depends, must be, and will be, either accepted or rejected.

But the conclusions toward which all the preceding analysis points include more than the insistence that our commitment to the individualism of democracy must be renewed. Almost as important, they also include the insistence that individualism will have to be reunderstood and re-expressed, that the whole "language" which we use to express it and to defend it and to incorporate it into our patterns of social institutions will have to be recast. Perhaps the simplest way to both dramatize and summarize these conclusions would be to rewrite the Declaration of Independence.

The relevant paragraph of this document is as follows. The numbers I have inserted in the text refer to the comparable parts of the translation I will present.

1 : We hold these truths to be self-evident,

2 : that all men are created equal,

3 : that they are endowed by their Creator with certain unalienable Rights, that among these are Life, Liberty, and the pursuit of Happiness.

4 : That to secure these rights, Governments are instituted among Men,

5 : deriving their just powers from the consent of the governed.

6 : That whenever any Form of Government becomes destructive of these ends, it is the Right of the People to abolish it, and to institute new Government, laying its foundation on such principles, and organizing its powers in such form, as to them shall seem most likely to effect their Safety and Happiness.

I am aware that to "rewrite," or, better, to translate into new terms, this paragraph may well seem pretentious. But I do not mean to be pretentious. I believe that I am aware of the historic significance of the Declaration and, as I said once before, I am as committed as any to the values for which it stands. Certainly I have no intention of even attempting to match Jefferson's rhetoric. But if I am myself convinced by all the arguments which I have set out in the preceding chapters, then I should be willing to demonstrate as vividly as possible the extent to which those arguments demand a recasting of some of our usual ways of looking at things. More than that. To translate this portion of the Declaration into new terms will provide one clear measure, though only one, of the kind of changes in our ways of thinking which I recommend. Finally, to rewrite or translate this paragraph will be the sharpest kind of demonstration of what I have been attempting in this book, to provide a new and more adequate exposition and defense of democratic individualism.

1 : We hold to these propositions as result of our commitment to the often contradictory values of the democratic way of life—

2 : that all men, while they are each members of particular societies, are also all members, under God, of the Brotherhood of Man, and are therefore all to be respected as moral agents, as men who can, and must, *do;*

3 : that, as members of the Brotherhood of Man, they are obliged to pursue a private occupation but that, as members of particular societies, they are simultaneously obliged to participate and serve in these; that, in short, they are private men with public duties;

4 : that, to secure the opportunities to pursue these divergent occupations, democratic citizens must look first to the states, instituted in their societies;

5 : that these states derive their moral legitimacy from the wisdom and skill with which they create and maintain systems of political obligations and political rights to enable and to leave free the citizens to fulfill their callings both public and private;

6 : that, when a state fails to provide such a system of obligations and rights, or does so but inefficiently, the citizens are morally obligated, by their commitment to the values inherent in the democratic faith and especially to the individualism which is the vital center of that faith, to abolish that state, to reform it, or otherwise to protest against it in such manner and to such degree as may be possible and necessary to bring about the required changes.

NOTES

NOTES

PREFACE

1 : G. H. Sabine, *A History of Political Theory*, New York, 1937 (2nd ed., 1949), p. vii.
2 : *Ibid.*, p. viii.
3 : *Ibid.*
4 : In his Introduction to Carl Becker, *Freedom and Responsibility,* New York, 1949.
5 : E.g., Sabine, *op. cit.*, and C. H. McIlwain, *The Growth of Political Thought in the West,* New York, 1932. More specifically, McIlwain's ideas on the significance of the Old and New Testaments to Western political theory are typical of what was for a long time the dominant point of view. McIlwain's position is that early Jewish political traditions were purely theocratic with a later tendency toward monarchy. However, he admits that more importance should be attached to the fact that "political controversialists from the fourth to the eighteenth century" regularly cited the Old Testament books in support of their arguments. "As such the early political history of the Jews is a subject of great importance for the history of political thought as a whole" (p. 147). As for the New Testament, McIlwain finds that it offers such a confusion of possible arguments for political theory that he, at least, does not feel justified in drawing any conclusions about its political influence at

245

all. In terms of formal political theory very strictly defined, the older scholars such as Sabine and McIlwain probably were right to minimize the influence on political ideas of Christianity as a religion. Substantively and generally they could not, it seems to me, have been either more blind or wrong, especially with respect to the development of Western democratic theory.

CHAPTER I

1 : A. W. Dunn, "Civic Education in . . . Indianapolis," U. S. Bureau of Education Bulletin 1915, No. 17; D. J. Pugh, "The Validation of a Technique for Measuring . . . Civic Attitude . . ." (Ph.D. Dissertation), Ithaca, N. Y., 1940; T. J. Morgan, *Patriotic Citizenship*, New York, 1895; E. A. Weber, *The Duk-Duks* (one of a series of eleven studies in *The Making of Citizens* covering nine countries), Chicago, 1921. This list is hardly even a sample of the titles available.

2 : J. W. Gates, "The Civic Competence of High School Seniors," in *Chicago Dissertations* No. 216 (1945).

3 : E.g., The Read Report, "Preparing College Men and Women for Politics," the Citizenship Clearing House, New York, 1950.

4 : J. S. Mill, *On Liberty*, Everyman's Lib. ed., London, 1910, p. 67.

5 : For an example and discussion of these techniques of word analysis, see M. Cranston, *Freedom, A New Analysis*, London, 1953, Pt. I.

6 : Michael Oakeshott, *Political Education*, Cambridge, England, 1951, p. 28.

CHAPTER II

1 : Of these A. E. Zimmern, *The Greek Commonwealth*, 3rd ed. rev., Oxford, 1922, is perhaps the classic.

2 : E. Barker, "Introduction" to his translation of *The Politics of Aristotle*, Oxford, 1946, pp. lxiii–lxvii. The definitions given above are paraphrases of Barker's comments.

3 : *Ibid.*, p. lxiii.

4 : The robot qualities of the modern legislative member are relevant neither to the present argument nor to the kind of direct democracy which the Athenians had. They are explicable only

in terms of theories of party and representative government—
theories with which the Greeks can be said to have had any
familiarity only by pushing the evidence available very hard
indeed.

5 : This, of course, is not to suggest that citizenship destroys the
family or even seeks to. But it does tend to break it up from
one generation to the next and certainly displaces it as a center
of social loyalty. For the citizen, the family is "back home" and
for his city it is primarily the nursery of new citizens.

6 : Thucydides, *History of the Peloponnesian War,* trans. B. Jowett,
in *The Greek Historians,* ed. F. R. B. Godolphin, New York,
1942, I, 653.

7 : C. D. Burns, *Greek Ideals,* London, 1917, p. 64.

8 : Zimmern, *op. cit.,* p. 60, n. 2.

9 : J. B. Bury, *A History of Greece,* 3rd ed. rev. R. Meiggs, London,
1951, p. 187.

10 : *Politics,* p. 117.

11 : *Ibid.,* p. 205.

12 : Zimmern, *op. cit.,* pp. 61–65.

13 : Locke, who saw possession of Reason as the grounds for granting men liberty, may also be suspected of making exceptions
of this same, "illogical" sort (viz., *2nd Treatise,* Chaps. 5 and
6 on Property and Paternal Power). But Locke's seventeenth-
century middle-class prejudices are effectively concealed from
us by the tradition that he was a great democrat—in *our* sense
of the word—and by the fact that most of us have middle-
class prejudices too.

14 : Burns, *op. cit.,* p. 69.

15 : Thucydides, *op. cit.,* p. 648.

16 : In an interview on the occasion of his eightieth birthday, *New
York Times,* March 26, 1954, p. 23, col. 5.

17 : Burns, *op. cit.,* p. 75.

18 : Zimmern, *op. cit.,* pp. 169–170, note.

19 : *Politics,* p. 95.

20 : *Leviathan,* ed. M. Oakeshott, Oxford, n.d., p. 64.

21 : Johs. Pedersen, *Israel, Its Life and Culture,* trans. from the
Danish by the author & Mrs. Aslaug Møller, Oxford, 1926, pp.
108–109.

22 : *Ibid.,* pp. 100–101.

23 : I Kings 18: 44.

24 : A. R. Johnson, *The Vitality of the Individual in the Thought of Ancient Israel,* Cardiff, 1949, p. 89.

25 : I Kings 1: 1–4.

26 : This is the more accurate rendering—though, since only the consonants YHWH were employed in the original manuscripts, the vowel sounds are uncertain. "Jehovah," the more familiar rendering, dates from the late medieval period and is a hybrid of "Yahweh" and the vowels of the word "Adonai," meaning Lord.—H. H. Rowley, *The Growth of the Old Testament,* London, 1950, p. 24; Preface, R.S.V., New York, 1953, pp. iv–v.

27 : Exod. 34: 14–15.

28 : Pedersen, *op. cit.,* p. 165.

29 : *Ibid.,* p. 130.

30 : Exod. 24: 4–8.

31 : W. O. E. Oesterley & T. H. Robinson, *Hebrew Religion, Its Origin and Development* (2nd ed. rev.), London, 1937, pp. 156–157.

32 : Much of the argument of this and the preceding paragraphs is based on Rousseau's *Social Contract* (trans. G. D. H. Cole, Everyman's Lib. ed., London, 1913), particularly on Bk. II, Chap. 3 and Bk. III, Chap. 2, where attempts are made to distinguish between and relate "private will," "The will of all," and "The General Will." The argument which advanced most the concept of the Living State was that, of course, of G. F. Hegel in *The Philosophy of Right* (trans. T. M. Knox, Oxford, 1942). T. H. Green, in *Lectures on Political Obligation* (London [1900], 1941 ptg.), is the Liberal who, while accepting the definition of man as will, the citizen as therefore loyal, struggles hardest, and not altogether unsuccessfully, against the totalitarian implications of the resultant social theory. Reference should also be made to Hobbes, *Leviathan* (ed. M. Oakeshott, Oxford, n.d.), especially to pp. 87 ff. on contracts; pp. 105 ff. on things personated; pp. 166 ff. on the distinction between counsel and command and the nature of obedience; and p. 112 on the generation of "that mortal god," the commonwealth.

CHAPTER III

1 : Some might prefer for "private occupation" the term "vocation" as being more usual in this connection. But "private occupation" becomes for the rest of this book a set phrase designating a general pattern of ideas within which the actual occupation prescribed can be variously defined. For this purpose, "vocation" is too narrowly associated with orthodox forms of Christian experience.

2 : Exod. 20: 12. *N.B.* This commandment is, of course, no more— and no less—prudential than the search by many moderns for "peace of mind" through performance of one or another religious exercise.

3 : Amos 1: 1; 6: 1–4.

4 : Jer. 18: 6–7.

5 : Jer. 12: 1.

6 : It is tempting to suggest that Jeremiah in this passage is also personal in the sense that he is asking questions about the consequences to individuals of their personal wrongdoing. But this would be reading too much into a little. There is only slight evidence in Jeremiah, though there is ample in Ezekiel as I shall be noting in a moment, of a sense of personal responsibility and, in any case, the context of the present passage makes clear that the "wicked" referred to are not particular individuals but the whole House of Israel. *N.B.* See below, note 10, for a discussion of Jeremiah's foretelling of a "new covenant" and its significance to the development of personal concerns in Hebraic religion.

7 : Jer. 29: 7.

8 : *Supra,* p. 45.

9 : *Supra,* pp. 63–70.

10 : Ezek. 18: 1–4 and 19–20. Compare the words in Deut. 5:9, written hardly more than a generation earlier, which talk of "visiting the sins of the fathers upon the children, and upon the third and upon the fourth generation of them that hate me."— Quoted in W. O. E. Oesterley & T. H. Robinson, *Hebrew Religion,* 2nd ed. rev., London, 1937, p. 292.

A passage very similar to this one in Ezekiel also appears in Jeremiah. It cites the same proverb about sour grapes and says that it shall be heard no more. The conclusion that sin is a personal matter is put and, if anything, more succinctly than in Ezekiel: "But every one shall die for his own iniquity: every man that eateth the sour grape, his teeth shall be set on edge."—Jer. 31: 30. Immediately following these words is the announcement: "Behold, the days come, saith the Lord, that I will make a new covenant with the house of Israel, and with the house of Judah." Details of this new covenant are not given except that it will be written "in their hearts" so that all men, "from the least of them unto the greatest of them," will know the Lord immediately without having to be told about Him. It can be argued, therefore, on the basis of these passages, that it was Jeremiah, not Ezekiel, who first put the problem of personal redemption. For the generality of my argument, it is not important to settle this. It is enough to show that in the prophets of the Exile, however tentatively, a relationship between individual men and a universal god was being sometime assumed (this certainly is the major feature of Jeremiah's new covenant) and that, within that relationship, a problem of personal nature was sometimes being postulated. I have used Jeremiah to develop the first of these points and Ezekiel the second partly for simplicity of exposition but also because in Jeremiah this passage on the individuality of sin is so brief whereas in Ezekiel the comparable passage is relatively extensive, because in Jeremiah the insistence is that the day *will* come when God will judge men individually whereas in Ezekiel the assumption is that He has already begun to judge in this way, and lastly because in Jeremiah it is at least ambiguous whether he means each man or each generation will be judged on earned merit whereas in Ezekiel there is no such ambiguity. To take matters further than this would not advance my general argument at all and would in addition involve me deeply in hotly debated questions about the date and authorship of the numerous sections of these books.

11 : Isa. 7: 14; 9: 2–7; 11: 12; 14: 2.
12 : Matt. 16: 16; Mark 8: 29; Luke 9: 20.
13 : Mark 8: 33.
14 : Matt. 5: 17.
15 : John 1: 17.

16 : Matt. 5: 3–8, 27–28; 6: 5–6.

17 : Matt. 5: 3–16.

18 : Matt. 5: 17–48.

19 : Matt. 22: 15–22; Mark 12: 13–17; Luke 20: 19–26.

20 : Acts 15: 1–35; Gal. 2: 11–14.

21 : I Cor. 12: 4, 6, 12.

22 : Some of this advance in Plebeian status was due to Patrician efforts to ensure Plebeian support. As early as the fifth century B.C., the Patricians began a reorganization of the army which, while guaranteeing that control still remained in their hands, yet demanded money and service from all in the city. The Patricians also granted certain commercial rights to the Plebs. On the other hand, the Plebs knew their worth and, in that knowledge, demanded improvement in their status. They obtained, over a long period of struggle, legal recognition of their civil acts. They forced the adoption of the Twelve Tablets, a body written law which superseded the merely oracular law which previously the Patrician magistrates had applied to them. By the "Secession to the Sacred Mount" in 492 B.C., the Plebs secured the establishment of the office of Tribune and also of an assembly of their own, the Assembly of Tribes. Later, they gained both recognition that acts of this assembly were binding on all citizens and admission to the formal assembly of the Roman state of that period, the *Comitia Curiata*. With these victories, in time, came also admission to the Senate and to the important magistracies including the Consulships.

23 : In the *Comitia Tributa*, the descendant of the old Plebeian Assembly of Tribes, voting was by tribes, of which, after the middle of the third century, there were 35. But the tribes were grossly unequal in size. The 4 Urban tribes were much the largest and into them were poured all the new citizens created by the manumission of slaves. Admission of other new citizens was allowed into only about half of the 31 Rustic tribes. The situation in *Comitia Centuriata*, the army assembly, was more complex but even more effective in reserving power to the established and rich. There voting was by centuries within classes, admission to which was on a graduated basis of wealth. In all, there were 373 centuries distributed through 7 classes. At one extreme were the knights, the wealthiest class, which comprised in all less than 2,000 citizens, but they were organ-

ized into 18 centuries and therefore had in the assembly 18 votes. At the other extreme were the some 130,000 proletarians, citizens who did not have the wherewithal to buy admission into even the lowest of the regular classes of the army. And they were lumped all together into 1 century and therefore could exercise between them all only 1 vote. These and other arrangements ensured that on the great issues which came before the *Comitia Centuriata,* including that of war and peace, three out of four of all those technically eligible to participate were effectively disenfranchised.

24 : These rights were primarily civil. The rights of a criminally accused of the sort with which we are familiar today are almost wholly the product of the English common law tradition. In Rome, the problem of social discipline was handled first by *pater familias* and then passed more and more into the hands of the imperial administrators rather than the courts.

25 : Except for a class called *dediticii,* a technical term the meaning of which is apparently unknown. The number included in it is supposed to have been absolutely considerable but relatively very small. The reason for their exclusion is not known. There may have been some slight increase in the revenues of the state as a result of this decree. But it is thought that Caracalla's own immediate reason for issuing it was that he needed to distract attention from the cold-blooded and dishonorable means he had used to gain full possession of the power from his brother. Caracalla had arranged a meeting with his brother and their mother to settle the quarrel for power, and when the brother arrived, Caracalla had the poor man murdered even as he sought protection in their mother's arms.

26 : Gal. 2: 15–16.

27 : II Thess. 3: 10–13; cf. I Cor. 12: 27–31.

28 : Gal. 3: 26–28; cf. I Cor. 12: 12–13.

29 : Eph. 3: 8–9; 4: 4–6.

30 : *Confessions* (trans. E. B. Pusey), Mod. Lib. No. 263, 1949, p. 69.

31 : *Ibid.,* pp. 128–129.

CHAPTER IV

1 : Abraham Lincoln, "The Gettysburg Address," in *Selected Speeches, Messages, and Letters,* Rinehart Editions, New York, 1957, p. 246.
2 : James Madison, *The Federalist, No. X,* Oxford, 1948, pp. 41–48.
3 : Elbert Hubbard, "A Message to Garcia," in *Democracy and the Gospel of Wealth,* ed., G. Kennedy, Boston, 1949, p. 87.
4 : H. D. Thoreau, "On Civil Disobedience," in Rinehart Editions, New York, 1948, p. 290.
5 : J. S. Mill, *On Liberty,* Everyman's Lib. ed., London, 1910, pp. 72–73.

INDEX

INDEX

257